THE STRENGTH
OF A MAN

Discovery House Publishers

Books, music, and videos that feed the soul with the Word of God

Box 3566 Grand Rapids, MI 49501

THE
STRENGTH
OF A MAN

David Roper

To my wife Carolyn,
who makes me want to be a man.

The Strength of a Man
Copyright © 1989 by David Roper

Discovery House Publishers is affiliated with RBC Ministries,
Grand Rapids, Michigan 49512

Discovery House books are distributed to the trade by
Thomas Nelson Publishers, Nashville, Tennessee 37214

Unless indicated otherwise, Scripture is taken from the
HOLY BIBLE, NEW INTERNATIONAL VERSION.
Copyright © 1973, 1978, 1984 International Bible Society.
Used by permission of Zondervan Bible Publishers.

Library of Congress Cataloging-in-Publication-Data

Roper, David, 1933–
  The strength of a man : encouragement for today / by David Roper
    p. cm.
  ISBN: 0-929239-07-5

  1. Meditations. I. Title.
BV4832.2.R65 1989
242'.642—dc19   89-1180
                                    CIP

Printed in the United States of America

97 98 99 00 01 02 / CHG / 20 19 18 17 16 15 14 13 12 11

CONTENTS

FOREWORD

The veteran apostle Paul wrote to young Timothy, who was trying to keep spiritually afloat in Ephesus, and addressed him as "Man of God." It must have spoken volumes to young Timothy's heart to know that his great mentor saw him in that light, despite his struggles. It is always marvelously encouraging to know that someone knows you and believes in you. So these words from the pen of David Roper will greatly enhearten those who seek to be men of God in these pressure-ridden days. For, as Dave says in his introduction, "I love men and I want to see them come into their own."

Our church in Palo Alto still is being impacted by the men whom David Roper reached and discipled when he served on our pastoral staff. His work as College Pastor bore great fruit on the campus of Stanford University, and it is no surprise to me to see his present ministry as pastor of Cole Community Church in Boise reaching out to touch much of the state.

Few expositors have the ability, as David has, to open up a verse or even a phrase from Scripture and make it gladden the heart—or explode like a bomb in the brain! There is a freshness and honesty about David's comments that always remind me of Oswald Chambers and his much-used *My Utmost for His Highest*. I predict that what Chambers did for my generation, Roper will do for the men of today's world.

—Ray C. Stedman

THE MEANING
OF MAN

Most of my friends consider themselves real men. They're outdoorsmen and sportsmen. They hunt and fish. They hang their snowmobiles upside down under the snow cornices on West Mountain. They hie themselves across the desert in 4X4s at what I consider terminal velocities. I have one friend who pulled a grizzly bear off of his wife with his bare hands. I saw another ride a log down a canyon wall. He almost broke the sound barrier on the way down; he did break two ribs at the bottom. But to hear him tell it, it was the thrill of a lifetime.

Yet for all our macho, we men are uneasy about our manhood. None of us seems to know for sure what it means. We have to be told: Real men don't eat quiche. They never bunt. They don't have "meaningful dialogues." And rarely do they think about the meaning of life. Real men love John Wayne, Monday Night Football, chain saws, and Coors.

These efforts to define our manhood are funny; they spoof the affectation and humbug with which we support our sagging male egos. Avoiding quiche is a good symbol of our uncertain sexuality. But what impresses me most is that it's done, that we find it necessary to be told what it means to be a man. Our ignorance must be a measure of our confusion. Few of us understand that true manhood is not a matter of power displays and aggressiveness; it is a function of the activity of God. In the beginning it took God to make a man, and it still does.

We have a lot to learn about being men. I know I do. I doubt that many of our hunting and fishing buddies, for all their high jinks and good humor, can help us much. But there is One, the manliest man of all, who invites us to learn from Him. He wrote the book on the subject, the manual that goes with man. I offer some thoughts on that book and what it reveals about man. I share them because I love men and I want to see them come into their own.

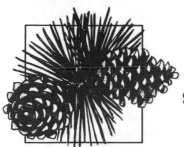

SATISFACTION

Warm-up: Psalm 42–43

My soul thirsts for God,
for the living God. When
can I go and meet with
God? (Ps. 42:2).

A friend of mine turned forty recently and immediately took leave of his senses. He left his wife of twenty years, got a perm, a Porsche, a synthetic suntan, and moved in with his twenty-two-year-old girlfriend. I have nothing against perms, tans, or sports cars, but I just wondered why he did it. Forty seems much too old to start over; I keep thinking of Nicodemus's question, "Can a man be born when he is old?" (John 3:4).

It's just the flesh, I thought at first. Nothing more than high jinks or high-handed sinning. But the way he went about it, so joylessly, resolutely, and methodically, made me think further. It was as though he was mindlessly following a script. And then I recalled other friends who had done the same thing. What causes this forty-year itch? Maybe it's a kind of male menopause, a time in a man's life when his hormones run amok and he acts as though he's been dropped on his head from a great height. But I could think of no hard medical evidence for that conclusion. At least nothing I'd read on the subject sounded very convincing.

Another friend explained his great escape by speaking of the need for self-fulfillment and personal well-being. "I have a duty to myself," he intoned. Yet it was hard for me to believe that he had jettisoned all his old values out of some strange moral principle that he ought to deny himself nothing. Certainly he knew better than that. And anyway, he argued too loud and too long in his own defense. I wondered whom he was trying to convince.

Another left out of sheer boredom. As he put it, he had a successful business, a charming house, a smiling wife, three kids, and a seven handicap. He must have arrived. What bothered him most was the sterile sameness of it all, the feeling that there were no options left. Time like a wind had blown down the corridors of his life slamming and locking all the doors. He was trapped; there was no exit. To hear him tell it, the road was gentle and gradual, no milestones or signposts. He just woke up one morning and realized that, like Alexander the Great, he had won; nothing was left to conquer. He had everything he ever wanted, but he wanted nothing he had.

Still another got the itch when it occurred to him that he would never arrive. He always envisioned himself climbing the organizational ladder, but as he aged, a gnawing desperation set in.

As Lucy says, "Winning isn't everything; winning *big* is!" Most of us need to win big. The problem, however, is that there seems to be a law of diminishing returns: the bigger wins give a decreasing measure of satisfaction.

The Bible says we're cursed. The ground yields a high proportion of thorns and thistles. Our work often frustrates us and payday never delivers enough. The itch remains that cannot be scratched. It's then that we start thinking about a way to opt out or at least to escape the pain. Turning over a new leaf doesn't work well; we don't achieve more the second time around. And there are, of course, only a finite number of times we can go around before we run out of time.

God offers a better way to satisfy our longings. Our unsatisfying searches reveal our need of Him. Augustine was right: "Our hearts are restless until they find rest in him. We were made for God and nothing else will do. He is the only end to our search."

God stimulates in us a profound hunger that is nothing less than the answering cry of our hearts to God's wooing. Because He loves us, He won't let us alone. He interrupts and interferes, hectoring us, hounding us with an infinite unrest.

We sense a divine discontent as God's love pushes, pulls, prods, and nudges us closer to Him. He goads us on almost irresistibly. As God Himself told Paul, "It is hard . . . to kick against the goads!" (Acts 26:14).

But some will ask, "Why can't He mind His own business and leave us alone?" He won't because we are His business. He loves us with relentless love; He will not rest until we're His.

To say we'll only have complete satisfaction in God strikes us as too simple, but the simplest answers reveal the profoundest truths. Until we find our peace in Him, we'll continue to feel alone, caught in midlife crisis and forever itching.

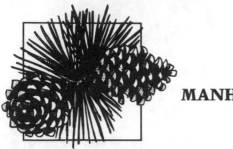

MANHOOD

*What is man that you
are mindful of him?*
(Ps. 8:4).

I must confess that I'm a humanist—like David who wrote the eighth Psalm. His poem raises the best question of all: "What is man?"

What is man? Biologically, he's a mammalian vertebrate; order: primate; genus: homo; species: sapiens. His body is made up of organs, tissues, cells, and protoplasm. Chemically, he's composed mostly of water, a large quantity of carbon, and various amounts of iron, calcium, magnesium, phosphorus, sulpher, lime, nitrogen, and some mineral salts. Psychologically, he has intellectual, emotional, and volitional powers and various instincts. He has on occasion dashed off a 4.2-second forty and leaped into the air a little over 7½ feet.

But man has to be something more. We long for other, more complete explanations. Something in man refuses to be cribbed and confined and reaches out beyond mere scientific description. Eternity is in our hearts. We too ask, "What is man? What am I?"

Down inside us is a mystery from which comes our pursuit of excellence, our love of athletics, art, and music, our yearning to know and to be known, our deep discontent at our inability to live up to our own ideals. This is part of the "something more" that makes us truly human. That's why we want to know what it means to be a man.

We ask, as Saul Bellow did, "Is there nothing else between birth and death but what I can get out of this perversity—only a favorable balance of disorderly emotions? No freedom? Only impulses? And what about all the good I have in my heart—doesn't it mean anything? Is it simply a joke? A false hope that makes a man feel the illusion of worth?" Is this all there is?

And what about our instincts? We know that men were meant to be courageous, selfless, loyal. Manhood is deeply rooted and is a memory written in our hearts. We know the rules. We just can't comply. And in the end we get tired of trying to be a man. As G. K. Chesterton said, "Pessimism comes not when we get weary of doing evil but when we get weary of doing good." No, there must be something more.

What are we? The psalmist fills in the picture. God made man the summit of creation, the highest order of created beings, only slightly less than God Himself, the most godlike creature in heaven and earth. Man is the only creature who shares God's glory and honor. We have great dignity and worth. For all our foibles and flaws, we have vast potential for good in science and technology, in arts and letters. We have tremendous capacity to give and love, to know and to be known. No man has ever plumbed his own depths. We're wonderful because God made us so.

The poet's conclusion, therefore, is noteworthy: "O LORD, our Lord, how majestic is *your name* in all the earth!" (v.9, italics mine). His contemplation of man's greatness leads the poet to worship not man but the God who made him, who "crowned him with glory and honor," and "put everything under his feet."

And so we, along with the poet, give thanks to the One who made man—who formed the creative genius of Michelangelo, the musical genius of Amadeus Mozart, the hand-eye coordination of Joe Montana. Contrary to our common belief, there are no self-made men. "It is he that hath made us, and not we ourselves" (Psalm 100:3, KJV). We know that it takes God to make men great, and we give thanks to Him for making us what we are. We must give credit where credit is due.

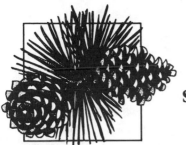

SOLITUDE

Warm-up: Psalm 63

*He went up on a
mountainside by himself
to pray. When evening
came, he was there alone
(Matt. 14:23).*

I've often thought of myself as mismatched for my job. People fill my days, and yet I'm not a people-person at all. I could easily have been a monk.

The backcountry saves me, I tell myself. I'm an Idahoan by call and a fly fisherman by choice—a happy arrangement where call and choice coincide. And so when the pressure gets to be too much or people get to be too many, I grab my fly rod and head for the hills. There are times when I have to be alone!

I've often encouraged myself with the thought that Jesus Himself wanted to be alone. After all, doesn't the Gospel say so? "He went up on a mountainside by himself to pray. When even came, he was there alone" (Matt. 14:23). If He, the Son of God, needed solitude, how much more do I! But Jesus did more than spend time alone; He expended the hours in solitude with God.

Henri Nouwen mentions a conversation with Mother Teresa of Calcutta. When he asked how he could better order his life, she replied with characteristic simplicity: "Spend one hour a day in adoration of our Lord and you'll be alright." I'm sure she would say there's nothing sacred about the amount of time one spends. That may vary from person to person. It's the principle that matters; *well-being grows out of worship.*

Most of us overdose on everything; we get caught up in the system, doing things without our hearts in them. The only solution is to get back in touch with God and recreate our first love by creating time for Him. As James said, "Draw near to God and He will draw near to you" (James 4:8, NASB). Centering on God gives us His perspective on everything and His power to serve. Without Him our lives become dull and sterile, and in the end a bore.

A friend of mine suggested a helpful analogy. He said that our spirituality is a lot like like trying to stay on a playground merry-go-round. The closer one gets to the center the easier it is to hold on. The essential thing, then, is to center on God.

Most men are far too busy to make that much room in their lives for God. We have things to do, "promises to keep, miles to go before we sleep." And yet when the day is done, what do we have to show but bankrupt enthusiasm and emptiness? What's been done that matters?

What's needed is more of God in us and a quiet time and place in which to draw near to God and He to us. An older generation of Christians might have thought in terms of withdrawal from the world. They would have gone to the desert or entered a monastic order to find a place and time for the quiet life. Although the Reformation rescued us from the abuses of monasticism, the benefits continue. But where in our busy schedules can we find this place of quiet rest? As T.S. Eliot lamented,

"Where shall the word be found? Where will the word rebound? Not here, there is not enough silence."

Everyone has twenty-four hours each day. The issue is not what we do; it's the value assigned to everything done. We must distinguish between the essential and the merely urgent.

And so we need solitude, far from the madding crowd—not mere privacy but time alone with God, a regular specific time and place to read His Word, pray, worship, a beginning place from which we can practice God's presence through the day.

"Without solitude," Henri Nouwen wrote, "it is virtually impossible to live a spiritual life." Solitude begins with a time and place for God, and Him alone. If we really believe not only that God exists but also that He is actively present in our lives—healing, teaching, and guiding we must set aside a time and space to give Him our undivided attention. Jesus said, "Go into your room, close the door, and pray to your Father who is unseen" (Matt. 6:6).

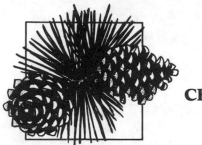

CHOOSING

Blessed are those who hunger and thirst for righteousness, for they will be satisfied (Matt. 5:6, NASB).

I received a letter from an old friend in Kenya. He's a pastor to pastors. It was a poignant note—an appeal for help.

"I want to know God," he wrote. "I want to love him. I want (as J. I. Packer speaks of it) to know the reality of the presence of Jesus Christ through the mediatorial work of his Holy Spirit. Yet I do not seem to want it enough, for I stand at the edge and merely look with longing. As someone said, the world is ablaze with God's glory, and only those with eyes to see take off their shoes. The rest sit around and pluck blackberries. I am, at present, a dissatisfied blackberry plucker, but I do not know how to take off my shoes. Help me at least to untie them!"

My reaction at first was John the Baptist's. Who am I to tie, much less untie, my friend's shoes? Given his vocational choice how can I doubt his love for Christ? But I know how he feels; I too struggle with the dross in my mind and the hardness of my heart.

A. W. Tozer once wrote, "God is a person who can be known in increasing degree of intimacy if we prepare our hearts for the wonder of it." There's the reality. God is a living person who can be known. But, ah, there's also the rub! We long for intimacy, but what we want doesn't amount to much. It's what we prepare ourselves for that matters. God responds to the slightest approach, but we're only as close as we want to be.

God isn't playing hard to get; He is not hard to find, but He will not foist His love on us. As Moses promised, "If . . . you seek the LORD your God, you will find him if you look for him with all your heart and with all your soul" (Deut. 4:29). Our progress toward God depends on our determination to know Him and love Him. It's a matter of choice.

The first thing, then, is to want God very much, as the psalmist did:

One thing I ask of the LORD,
this is what I seek:
that I may dwell in the house of the LORD
all the days of my life,
to gaze upon the beauty of the LORD
and to seek him in his temple (Ps. 27:4).

As long as we have only a vague discontent with our present way of living and only an indefinite desire for spiritual things, our lives will continue to stagnate into melancholy. We often say, "I'm not happy; I'm not really joyful or peaceful; I guess that's the way life is." It's this mood of resignation that keeps us from actively searching for the life of God. Our first task is to dispel that vague feeling of discontent and get honest with ourselves. Do we want God in us or not? It's a matter of enthusiasm—what lights up our eyes. Augustine said, "The entire life of a good Christian is nothing less than holy desire."

We should also persist in the pursuit of God through devotion and worship, regularly reading the Word and watering it with prayer, praise, adoration, and meditation day and night.

We should be willing to deal with defilement. Present sin, persisted in, obscures our vision of God. As Jesus said, "Blessed are the pure in heart, for they [and they alone] will see God" (Matt. 5:8). Sin substitutes one thirst for another; it limits our intimacy with God.

And then we should wait. Delay is an inevitable part of the process. Paul encouraged us not to get weary in doing good, "for at the proper time we will reap a harvest if we do not give up." The harvest doesn't come at the end of the day. It comes later.

F. B. Meyer wrote, "So often we mistake God and interpret his delays as denials. What a chapter might be written of God's delays. It is the mystery of educating human spirits to the finest temper of which they are capable. What searchings of the heart, what analyzings of motives, what testings of these weary days of waiting which are, nevertheless, big with spiritual destiny. But such are not God's final answer to the soul that trusts him."

The world sees no salvation in waiting but intimacy with God cannot be packaged and promised on time. "All holy desires heighten in intensity with the delay of fulfillment, and desire which fades with delay was never holy desire at all" (St. Gregory).

Good intentions are one thing; holy desire is another. We must have a will to wait. But His promise is good; He draws near to us as we draw near to Him (James 4:8). There's still this promise of reward that, as Oliver Goldsmith said, "reproves each dull delay."

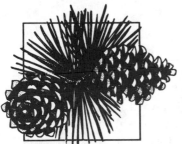

MOTIVES

Warm-up: Acts 8:4–24

*May your money perish
with you, because you
thought you could buy
the gift of God with
money (Acts 8:20).*

The good news was gaining ground: "Those who had
been scattered [from Jerusalem] preached the word wherever they went" (Acts 8:4). Philip, one of those who had
been extruded, went down to a city in Samaria and began
to preach the gospel there. When the people heard Philip
speak, they "all paid close attention to what he said" (v.
6). God's power was demonstrated. Evil spirits were ex-
orcized; principalities and powers were put on notice;
even the devil himself came around.

He showed up in the person of Simon Magus, the Ma-
gician, who for a long time had worked his mischief on
the Samaritans, enchanting them with his black arts,
claiming to be someone great. His followers echoed his
arrogance. "This man is nothing less than God himself.
He is Power Personified!" (v. 10, paraphrase). The people
of Samaria gave *him* their attention. He loved being in
the center.

When Simon saw Philip's crowd and his own flock
forming around the young evangelist, he "believed" and

was baptized, and followed Philip wherever he went, fascinated by his power (v. 13). The "magic" drew him.

The apostles in Jerusalem heard what had happened in Samaria and sent Peter and John to shepherd the movement. When the two men arrived they saw what was needed and prayed for the believers there, laying hands on them so that they might receive the Holy Spirit. The Spirit was poured out, as He was on the day of Pentecost, with all the external signs of His coming. This was too much for Simon! He offered Peter money. "Give me this power," he demanded. "What will you take for the Spirit?" (v. 19, paraphrase).

Peter, a discerning man, saw through his motives. "You have no part or share in this ministry, because your heart is not right before God. Repent of this wickedness and pray to the Lord that he will forgive you for having such a thought in your heart. For I see that you are full of bitterness and captive to sin." "Pray . . . for me," Simon pled, "so that nothing you have said may happen to me" (vv. 20–24, paraphrase). The plea sounded good, but there was no heart in it. Simon feared the consequences, not the sin.

Simon never changed his mind. He couldn't forget the halcyon days when the crowds applauded him. Galled by Philip's popularity, obsessed by his love of notoriety, enslaved by a lust for power, he had to get back into the center again.

Simon disappears from Luke's story, but his name turns up in other histories. One of the earliest church fathers, Justin Martyr (A.D. 100–165), said that Simon continued to practice magic until he made the big time again. When he went to Rome they made him a god. Jerome (A.D. 340–420), adds another sad note to the record, quoting Simon: "I am the Word of God; I am the Comforter; I am the Almighty; I am all there is of God." According to early writers Simon became the archenemy of the church and the father of all heresy, showing how far a man will go to get back into the center.

We should ask about ourselves and the self-centered motives of our hearts. Do we cherish them or do they shame us? Has the Spirit of Truth entered them and is the work deep enough to make us ashamed of our Magus-like motives?

Are we intoxicated by attention too? Do we crave it more and more? Does man's praise make us happy and is silence and lack of attention something we cannot get over? If so, we should know that God is not mocked. Our motives are naked and open to Him with whom we have to do.

"Seek obscurity" was Fénclon's motto. Few there are that find it!

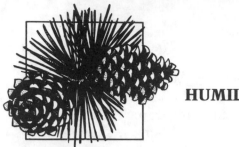

HUMILITY

Warm-up: Luke 14:1–11

*Whoever humbles
himself will be exalted
(Matt. 23:12).*

One of the vexing things about Jesus' teaching was His inclination to go too far and to push morality beyond what seemed to be feasible. Many of His sayings, as the disciples put it, were "hard." The simple teachings of Jesus often turned out to be not so simple after all.

One example is His teaching on humility, a trait which we find so hard to acquire but which he said was the highest good of all. "You are not to be called 'Rabbi' ['my master'] for you have only one Master and you are all brothers. And do not call anyone on earth 'father' for you have one Father, and he is in heaven. Nor are you to be called 'teacher' ['professor'] for you have one Teacher, the Christ. The greatest among you will be your servant. For whoever exalts himself will be humbled, and whoever humbles himself will be exalted" (Matt. 23:8–12).

In teaching about humility Jesus warned that we can take titles too seriously. Although we may appropriately use titles to identify people, we shouldn't let titles go to our heads. It costs too much and in the end may cost us everything. As He said, "Whoever exalts himself will be humbled."

This axiom about pride and humility occurred a number of times in Jesus' teaching (Matt. 18:4; 23:12; Luke 14:11; 18:14). It was a favorite saying of His; He must have meant it. He used it one Sabbath when dining with a prominent Pharisee. He noted how the guests picked out places of honor at the table and made the wry comment: "When someone invites you to a wedding feast, do not take the place of honor, for a person more distinguished than you may have been invited. If so, the host who invited both of you will come and say to you, 'Give this man your seat.' Then, humiliated, you will have to take the least important place. But when you are invited, take the lowest place, so that when your host comes, he will say to you, 'Friend, move up to a better place.' Then you will be honored in the presence of all your fellow guests. For everyone who exalts himself will be humbled, and he who humbles himself will be exalted" (Luke 14:8–11). Humiliation is the costly consequence of pride.

James discussed some consequences of pride; "Who is wise and understanding among you? Let him show it by his good life, by deeds done in the humility that comes from wisdom. But if you harbor bitter envy and selfish ambition in your hearts, do not boast about it or deny the truth. Such 'wisdom' does not come down from heaven but is earthly, unspiritual, of the devil. For where you have envy and selfish ambition, there you find disorder and every evil practice" (James 3:13–16).

In contrast, Paul said that our attitude "should be the same as that of Christ Jesus: Who being in very nature God, did not consider equality with God something to be grasped, but made himself nothing, taking the very nature of a servant, being made in human likeness. And being found in appearance as a man, he humbled himself and became obedient to death—even death on a cross! (Phil. 2:5–8).

C. S. Lewis pointed out that pride is the essential vice, the utmost evil. "Unchastity, anger, greed, drunkenness and all that are mere fleabites by comparison: it was through Pride that the devil became the devil. Pride leads to every other vice: it is the complete anti-God state of man." And because pride is the center of our resistance to God, God Himself resists it. As the apostle put it, "God opposes the proud but gives grace to the humble" (James 4:6). When we choose to be great, we forfeit God's grace.

On the other hand, humility, the opposite virtue, releases God's greatness. If pride leads to every other vice, humility leads to every other virtue. Humility is the basis of our life with God and our usefulness in this world. Thomas à Kempis wrote, "The more humble a man is in himself, and the more subject unto God; so much more prudent shall he be in all his affairs, and enjoy greater peace and quiet of heart."

If anyone wants to be humble, there's a way. The first step is to realize how proud we are. If we think we're humble, we're very proud indeed. Pride shows itself in subtle ways: insisting on recognition (our titles); wanting to be noticed, to be prominent and eminent; smarting when we're not consulted or advised on a matter; dominating social situations, telling our tales rather than listening to others; resisting authority; getting angry and defensive when crossed or challenged; harboring a grudge; nursing a grievance; wallowing in self-pity;

choosing our own kind rather than loving the lowly; wanting to be in the center rather than serving on the edge.

Pride also shows itself in those odd yearnings for bigger and better things. Why is God's will always upwardly mobile? Why is it so hard to stay with something small, where we're likely to be unnoticed and unknown? Why do we long for things more urban and urbane?

The best course, then, is to humble ourselves, to take the lowest place and the littlest place, to be content to be unknown and unnoticed, to refuse to dominate meetings and social situations, to be mostly silent, to listen more and say less and not insist that we be seen and heard, to choose to sit and associate with the lonely and the lowly (Rom. 12:16). To "take the lowest place" is the measure of a man.

And most important of all, we ought to draw near to Jesus and learn from Him because He was "meek and humble in heart," not the least bit concerned about protecting His place or His dignity (Matt. 11:29). "By meekness and defeat," wrote Samuel Gandy, "he won the mead and crown. Trod all his foes beneath his feet, by being trodden down." By coming again and again to Him, we'll become much more like Him, and we'll find rest for our souls—rest from all the posturing, pretending, and ambitious striving that keeps us so discontented and ill at ease.

Peter stated the same principle in another way: "Clothe yourselves with humility toward one another, because, 'God opposes the proud but gives grace to the humble.' Humble yourselves under the mighty hand of God that he may lift you up in due time" (1 Pet. 5:5–6). But the apostle added, significantly, "Cast all your anxiety on him because he cares for you" (v.7), and the context of this oft-quoted verse has to do with anxiety that comes from humbling ourselves and taking the lowest place. If I humble myself, if I put an end to my efforts to be seen and heard, if I don't look out for me, then who will? God will because He cares for me.

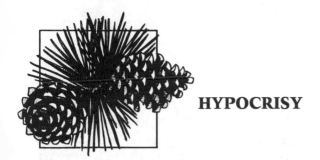

HYPOCRISY

*But didn't you drive out
the priests of the Lord,
the sons of Aaron, and
the Levites, and make
priests of your own as
the peoples of other
lands do? Whoever
comes to consecrate
himself with a young
bull and seven rams may
become a priest of what
are not gods (2 Chron.
13:9–10).*

Every man gets to be like his father, they say. That's his tragedy. Rehoboam is a case in point. Born a year or so before Solomon began to rule, Rehoboam was his father's favorite son and heir apparent. Seemingly he had every advantage, growing up in the court, learning the lessons of faith that would ready him to rule. But his father led him astray. As Solomon aged, he edged away from God. "He loved many foreign women . . ." and his wives led him away. It was a family sin that Solomon conferred on his son.

Unwilling to learn from his father's history, Rehoboam repeated it, and the verdict of Scripture is that, though he was a strong man with great potential, "He did evil because he did not set his heart on seeking the Lord" (2 Chron. 12:14). There was no end to his folly.

Rehoboam forsook the Word of God and the counsel of the elders and instead listened to his peers. He installed a Machiavellian, get-tough policy that tore the nation apart (2 Chron. 10). Then heeding the counsel of the queen mother, he reintroduced Baal worship into Judah. "The people engaged in all the detestable practices of the nations the LORD had driven out before the Israelites" (1 Kings 15:24). Reading the wrong books and listening to the wrong people led Rehoboam to do more evil than any of the kings that preceded him.

When "Rehoboam's position as king was established and he had become strong, he and all Israel with him abandoned the law of the Lord. Because they had been unfaithful to the Lord, Shishak king of Egypt attacked Jerusalem in the fifth year of Rehoboam. With twelve hundred chariots and sixty thousand horsemen and the innumerable troops of Libyans, Sukkites and Cushites that came with him from Egypt, he captured the fortified cities of Judah and came as far as Jerusalem" (2 Chron. 12:1–4).

The vast and powerful kingdom that Rehoboam inherited from his father Solomon was decimated. There was little left but ruin. Only Jerusalem remained, and that solely by God's grace. "My wrath shall not be poured out on Jerusalem because of Shishak. They will however become subject to him" (v. 8).

Rehoboam became the Pharaoh's vassal. Shishak's armies "carried off the treasure of the temple of the Lord and the treasures of the royal palace. He took everything, including all the gold shields Solomon had made." Rehoboam was ruined, bankrupted. Shishak's rape of Jerusalem was the righteous judgment of God.

"So King Rehoboam made *bronze* shields to replace them [the gold shields] and assigned these to the commanders of the guard on duty at the entrance to the royal palace. Whenever the king went to the Lord's temple, the guards went with him, bearing the shields, and afterward they returned them to the guardroom" (vv. 10–11). What about Rehoboam's ersatz shields? What was this "brazen" hoax?

Solomon's gold shields were a symbol for his day, representing the glory of his kingdom, a glory now gone. Rehoboam's kingdom was crumbling, but he kept on playing the game, "lookin' good" to the end. He trotted out his bogus shields on state occasions and displayed them for all to see and then concealed them in the guardhouse where no one could inspect them and expose his lie. It was a put-on. The glory was gone.

Rehoboam lives on in us when we've gone wrong and suffered for it and deny our loss; when we've forsaken the Lord and lost our place, but we try to look good to the end. We play the game and we pay the price in hesitation and fear. What if our sham is discovered? What if our cover is blown?

There's only one way back. We must stop conspiring and counterfeiting, admit our ruin, and face the facts of our lost rule. It's when we concede our sin and the consequences of it that God can begin to heal.

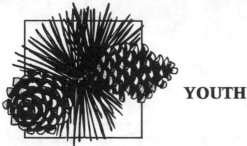

YOUTH

Warm-up: Ecclesiastes 11:9–12:8

*Don't let anyone look
down on you because
you are young, but set
an example for the
believers in speech, in
life, in love, in faith and
in purity (1 Tim. 4:12).*

"Youth is a marvelous time," said Shaw. "It's just too bad it's wasted on the young." Looking back, I have to agree. The best course is to make the most of your youth while you can.

The author-philosopher of Ecclesiastes was concerned with youth and their being the best that they could be. He concluded at one point:

Be happy, young man, while you are young,
and let your heart give you joy in the days of your
    youth . . .
banish anxiety from your heart
and cast off the troubles of your body,
for youth and vigor are meaningless (11:9–10).

"Banish anxiety"; don't be hassled! Why is it that young men and women are always bummed out about something or other? Love life! Live it to the limit! Ski the tough slopes, run the big rapids, pursue life with passion and élan! Go for broke! But

34

Remember your Creator
in the days of your youth
before the days of trouble come
and the years approach when you will say,
"I find no pleasure in them" (12:1).

Pleasure is one of life's deepest longings. We not only want to live; we want to live well. The good life is the only life worth living! We all have our schemes for making the most of life—a happy marriage, children, success, money, power, acclaim. But the distressing fact is that none of these accomplishments ever provide unqualified happiness. Something is always missing. There's always that nagging thought that there's got to be something more.

Furthermore, we spoil even brief periods of real enjoyment by fear, loneliness, worry, and disappointment. Even when we go all out in life, the secret of true satisfaction eludes us.

Jesus, on the other hand, knew how to live. He was a young man who lived life to the limit. He knew exactly who He was and what He was about. If He said something about a truly satisfying life, it would make sense to listen. "Now this is eternal life: that they may know you, the only true God, and Jesus Christ, whom you have sent" (John 17:3).

His words strike us both as familiar and far away. We know that a relationship satisfies us most in life—someone to hang around with. Friendship makes sense, though most of us have grown weary looking for a real friend.

Yet the relationship we may have tried all along to avoid is the one we've been looking for. The God whom we dread is actually the one we desire. And when we meet Him (or rather are met by Him), we find He is not at all what we thought He would be. He is the sum of everything good and true and beautiful.

He knows the entire universe and He knows each one of us! There isn't any crowd; everyone is special. He loves us and longs to bring His life to us—a dimension of life He calls "eternal," not so much to stress its duration as its quality. He imparts an eternal *kind* of life to us. The more we know of Him, the more truly alive we become.

So as the philosopher of old would say if he were around today, "Go for the gusto, but don't leave God out." He's the one who gives meaning to everything else. If we don't make room for Him, we'll surely become one of those who find no pleasure in life—one of the restless ones.

William Law said, "If you have not chosen God, it will make no difference in the end what you have chosen, for you have missed the purpose for which you were formed and you will have forsaken the only thing that satisfies."

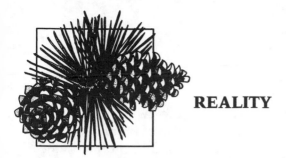

REALITY

Forgive my hidden faults
(Ps. 19:12).

I was fishing Lick Creek one day and cast my fly in a willow. It was the last of that pattern and the only one that was working. I said a very bad word. There are some things bad enough to make a preacher cuss, but my reaction suprised me. I hadn't used that word for a while; I wondered where it came from. But I was safe. Carolyn was fishing one hundred yards or so downstream; we were over one hundred miles away from my parish and twenty miles away from the nearest town; and there was no one around to hear.

Late that evening while I was attempting to set up the trailer, one piece of equipment would not work right. It was a warm, humid night and soon I was wringing wet and utterly frustrated. Carolyn tried to be helpful, offering advice since she couldn't offer anything else at the time.

I got annoyed and suggested that if she should like to try to start my car I would sit in her's and blow the horn. It's an old joke that she didn't find funny. Nor did I; I followed up with some angry words. Again, it surprised me; I rarely talked to her that way. But mostly I was chagrined because there *was* someone around to hear. I looked up from under the trailer into the eyes of two nearby kayakers who were taking in the whole scene. But once more I was safe; they were from California.

As Carolyn and I talked about the two incidents the next morning on the way back to Boise, I realized afresh that what I was in private was the real me. I had kidded myself into believing that my public image was what I was, but that was my illusion. The way I behave when there's no one around to hear or see is *me*! Everything else is a sham.

Dickens wrote about telescopic philanthropy—compassion for those at a distance but not for those at hand. I've always applied that principle to others, to those who decry apartheid but act as shamelessly as a South African bureaucrat toward those of other races in the United States. I don't apply the truth to myself. As Tolstoy said, "Everybody thinks of changing humanity and nobody thinks of changing himself."

I can talk about compassion for others and yet be utterly tactless and inconsiderate to my own family. In which case what I am at home is what I am. Or, I can think myself reasoned and self-controlled but what I do and say when angry and unobserved gives me away. And what I think in private is really me. My character is what I am when I'm alone.

I have a mountain friend who winters in a backcountry ranch all alone. He doesn't have a radio and doesn't read much. Most of the time he's snowed in. I asked him once what he did while he was there by himself. "Well," he mused, "I get to know myself real good." That sounded like wisdom then and it still does. If I would know myself well, I must know myself when I'm alone.

There's old Adam within, with vast potential for greed and selfishness. I know I can't change him much; frontal attack has never worked for me. As soon as I begin to resist sin, I endow it with more power. This same power it uses against me. Inner transformation, thus, is God's work. As Mother Teresa put it, we may *will* holiness, but He must do it.

What's needed is more of God in me. He must work His work. Righteousness is His gift, which I may receive. As David prayed, "Who can understand his wanderings? Forgive my hidden faults. Keep your servant also from [these] willful sins; may they not rule over me. Then I will be blameless, innocent of great transgression. May the words of my mouth and the meditation of my heart be pleasing in your sight, O Lord, my Rock and my Redeemer" (Ps. 19:12–14, paraphrase).

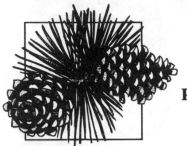

RETIREMENT

Warm-up: Joshua 14:1–15

*But my brothers who
went up with me made
the hearts of the people
melt with fear. I,
however, followed the
Lord my God
wholeheartedly (Josh.
14:8).*

Where have all the old men gone? Why do we get outdated and obsolete? Why are there so few over fifty on the cutting edge? Caleb, feisty old die-hard that he was, wouldn't understand. At 85 years of age, he stormed the heights—the ridge where the Anakites lived.

When Caleb was forty years old, Moses sent him with the spies to gather intelligence in the land of Canaan (Num. 13). They viewed the land and brought their report to the people. Canaan was indeed, as God had said, a land flowing with milk and honey. However, the Canaanites were strong, the cities were fortified, and the Anakites were there, the Titans of Hebron whose stature and strength were legendary.

Panic prevailed and paralyzed God's people, but Caleb drew out his faith. "We should by all means go up and take possession of the land, for we shall surely overcome it" (Num. 13:30, paraphrase). But the cynics shouted him down. "We are not able to go up against the people, for they are too strong for us" (v. 31, paraphrase). So, in unbelief, the people turned back at Kadesh-barnea and wandered away. Though pardoned by God they never entered the Land (vv. 20–35).

God said of Caleb, however, "Because my servant Caleb has a different spirit and follows me wholeheartedly, I will bring him into the land he went to, and his descendants will inherit it" (14:24). And so, this man, counting on that promise, counted the days, waiting for his chance. Like Milton's Abdiel: "Faithful among the faithless, only faithful he."

Forty-five years later, after the wilderness wanderings and the conquest of Canaan, Caleb stepped forward to claim his piece of ground. "Give me this hill country that the Lord promised me that day. You yourself heard then that the Anakites were there and their cities were large and fortified, but, the Lord helping me, I will drive them out just as he said" (Josh. 14:12). When most men would retire, Caleb kept on truckin'.

We ask, "What made this old veteran so young at heart? What kept him on the edge?" Three times we're told that he wholeheartedly followed the Lord God of Israel. Through pain and pressure, in spite of failings and flaws, through disappointment and delay, he made it his ambition to walk with God. Half-hearted men—those who fool around with personal ambition and enterprise and who make retirement their chief end—don't comprehend. They wither and die before their time. You see them around every town, dull and dreary old men with nothing to do, sitting on park benches or living on Park Avenue, with that dead look in their eyes—over the hill and never on top.

Not so Caleb. There was no stasis or stagnation in him. "From there [Hebron], Caleb drove out the three Anakites—Sheshai, Ahiman and Talmai—descendants of Anak" (Josh. 15:13). He thrashed the giants and drove them from the summit. He knew the secret of staying alive. Caleb *wholeheartedly* followed the Lord.

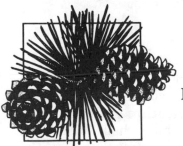

LONELINESS

Look to my right and
see; no one is concerned
for me. I have no refuge;
no one cares for my life
(Ps. 142:4).

Psalm 142 is a poem to wise us up. It's a Maskil (insightful psalm) of David. It was written in a cave.

David was being pursued by King Saul of Israel. When King Achish of Gath refused help, David found refuge in a cave near Adullam, a Canaanite city. Separated from family and friends, lost and unremembered, David blurted out his complaint:

I cry aloud to the Lord;
    I lift up my voice to the Lord for mercy.
I pour out my complaint before him;
    before him I tell my trouble.

When my spirit grows faint within me,
    it is you who know my way.
In the path where I walk
    men have hidden a snare for me.

Look to the right and see;
    no one is concerned for me (vv. 1–4).

43

The Strength of a Man

David was in trouble again. He wondered what God planned to do about it. The young would-be king had his share of enemies. Saul and his henchmen had isolated him in the desert and ambushed him—had "hidden an iron trap" for him there. But enemies were only half the story. It's one thing to have antagonists; it's quite another to have no friends. No one cared about David. No one "inquired" about him; no one knew his pain. He badly needed a friend.

But God gave David no earthly friends at this time but Himself. As David lamented, "It is you [alone] who know my way" (v. 3). Only God knew where David was; only God cared.

> I cry to you, O LORD;
>> I say, "You are my refuge,
>> my portion in the land of the living."
>
> Listen to my cry,
>> for I am in desperate need;
> Rescue me from those who pursue me,
>> for they are too strong for me.
>
> Set me free from my prison,
>> that I may praise your name.

We pray for friends and God denies us. His power seems to fail us; His stern denials thwart us. But behind that working is love controlling and a better purpose directing; and when we come to ourselves, stripped of every human resource, He gives us Himself, and we know Him to be the friend we've been wanting all along. As Richard Baxter said, "He wants not friends that hath Thy love."

And then, knowing that we've become God's friend we don't really *need* others. Others can lean on us rather than we on them. When we find our significance and security in Him, we can be a friend rather than want one.

> Then the righteous will gather around me
> because of your goodness to me.

When David found God to be friendly, he was soon surrounded with "friends": his needy family, righteous runaways, and renegades from Saul's ungodly regime. "Those who were in distress or in debt or discontented gathered round him," those who could do him no good. But he became their leader and their friend (1 Sam. 22:2), and so a better deed was done.

Annie Johnson Flint records her similar quest for a friend:

> I prayed for friends, and then I lost awhile
> All sense of nearness, human and divine;
> The love I leaned on failed and pierced my heart;
> The hands I clung to loosed themselves from
> mine;
> But while I swayed, weak, trembling and alone
> The everlasting arms upheld my own.
>
> I thank Thee, Lord, Thou wert too wise to heed
> My feeble prayers, and answer as I sought,
> Since these rich gifts Thy bounty has bestowed
> Have brought me more than I had asked or
> thought.
> Giver of good, so answer each request
> With Thine own giving, better than my best.

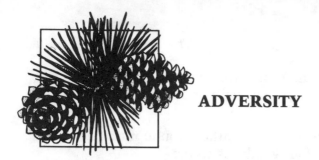

ADVERSITY

Warm-up: James 1:1–27

Consider it pure joy, my
brothers, whenever you
face trials (James 1:2–4).

Murphy's Law affirms: "If anything can go wrong it probably will." O'Toole's commentary on Murphy's Law alleges that Murphy was an optimist. I have to agree.

Things keep going wrong; adversity chases us. We hope that *someday* life will improve—when we marry, when we get out of school, when we get out of debt, when we retire—but our expectations never coincide with our realizations.

Since personal discomfort is inevitable, we ought to make the most of it and learn to suffer successfully. James explained: "Consider it pure joy, my brothers, whenever you face trials of many kinds, because you know that the testing of your faith develops perseverance. Perseverance must finish its work so that you may be mature and complete, not lacking anything" (James 1:2–4).

The supernatural reaction to adversity is *joy*, a word James used to imply contentment or well-being rather than mirth. When discomfort overtakes us we don't have to take to our beds or a bottle. We're okay.

The key to reacting with joy is to know that the pain of life is purposeful. Suffering has meaning; adversity is working for us, producing endurance.

Endurance is not mere resignation, tooth-clenched determination to tough it out to the end. That may be Stoic but it isn't Christian. James understood endurance as simple persistence, doing God's will in the face of counter-influences, forgiving slights and unkindness for the four hundred and ninetieth time, staying with a difficult marriage, struggling against enslaving habits, choosing purity of mind and body when to do so means lonely days and long nights, keeping one's word despite the pain of keeping it and obeying it when life is hard and when it hurts.

But the prospects aren't grim. Endurance yields a product—real men, tested and tough. Suffering makes us what George Fox called "established men"—stable, dependable, durable, and strong.

Unfortunately, our concept of God's goodness is based on the faulty assumption that personal happiness is the highest good. True happiness, however, is something more profound than staying in the comfort zone. There are things to be done about our character that can only be done by suffering. To shield us from this suffering would not be good; it would, in fact, rob us of the highest possible good.

And so our Lord permits suffering in order to mold us. Pain puts us on notice that we cannot do without God and pushes us closer to him; it shatters the illusion that we're adequate in ourselves. It draws us close to God and in Him we find the resources to face life and its demands. Without suffering we would never make the most of our manhood.

The Strength of a Man

That's why God seems careless about pain when it comes to his own. Disappointment, disenchantment, business, domestic, and financial problems are our lot. The way is strenuous, but on ahead is manliness.

When God wants to drill and skill a man;
When he wants to mold a man to play the noblest
    part.
When he yearns with all his heart to create so
    great and bold a man that all the world will be
    amazed.

How he ruthlessly perfects whom he royally
    selects.
How he hammers him and hurts him
    and with mighty blows converts him into trial
    shapes of clay which only God can understand.

How he bends but never breaks when his good he
    undertakes.
How he uses whom he chooses and with every
    purpose fuses him; by every act induces him to
    try his power out.

God knows what he's about!

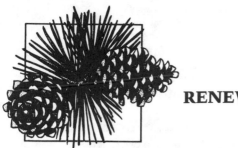

RENEWAL

Warm-up: Psalm 51

Have mercy on me, O God, according to your unfailing love; according to your great compassion blot out my transgressions. Wash away all my iniquity and cleanse me from my sin (Ps. 51:1–2).

God can take the worst that a man can do and make the best of it. *"Etiam peccatis* [Even from my sins]," wrote Augustine, God can draw good.

Think of David who stole his neighbor's wife and murdered the man to cover up the ghastly crime. But his sins were not overlooked. In time, they came home with terrible force, and David, utterly broken and repentant, prayed for God's mercy and cleansing.

David accepted God's forgiveness and got another start (v.10). "Then," he declared, "I will teach transgressors your ways, and sinners will turn back to you" (v. 13). David learned from his sin about God's compassion for the wayward and His tenacious pursuit to win them back. He discovered that God loves sinners though He hates their sin. He felt God's tenderness, and he taught God's tender ways to others. David's evil didn't undo him; he was much better for it.

Or consider Peter's blast of ego—"I'll go anywhere with you Lord!"—and his ultimate, awful denial (Luke 22:54–62).

Some years ago Carolyn, my wife, reflecting on Peter's failure, wrote this about her own shortcomings:

Lord, I start so strong
   saying "Anywhere!"
and I try to war and to defend you
   with sharpness and steel.

But Lord, I merely maim and wound;
   you alone can heal.
And then, bewildered in the mess,
   I start denying, all confused.

But Lord, that crowing in the night
   has jerked my spirit to attention.

And now I know (you knew it then)
   I'm weak,
      inept,
      cowardly,
      betraying,
      dust,
      guilty—just like him.

O Lord, compassionate and healing,
   you prayed then.

      And now I turn
         in humble weakness and
         in faith
      to worship you—and then to strengthen
   them.

   Hallowed be your name!

This is not to say that sin is good. Sin is sin and it leaves its scars on us, on others, and on God's heart. We shouldn't sin that good may come. Paul argues that only a fool would think that way (Rom. 6:1–14). But sin, repented of, can lead to greater good. All the wrong turns along the way, detours, the mistakes, the moral lapses, everything that seems irrevocably ugly, can make us better men if we allow it to lead us back to God.

So we must "forget what is behind and strain toward what is ahead" (Phil. 3:13). What's past is past. Dwelling upon the gravity of prior sin only leads to self-hatred and crippling guilt. Such thoughts are spawned by the father of lies. Our real Father forgives and works in all things for the glory and the good of those who love Him (Rom. 8:28).

He's the God of failures, frauds, and born losers. He loves us all, and He wants to make something of us. "By past history we are made more beautiful." Even from our sin God can draw good.

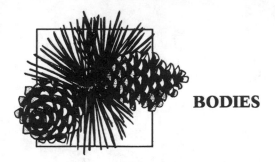

BODIES

Warm-up: 1 Corinthians 6:12–20

*The body is not meant
for sexual immorality,
but for the Lord, and the
Lord for the body . . .
Therefore honor God
with your body (1 Cor.
6:13, 20).*

In Paul's day, most philosophers believed that only the mind mattered, or more precisely, the things on which you put your mind mattered—the "Ideals." The body therefore was base and either you got it into line or you gave up on it and went for all the gusto. Stoic or Epicurean, monk or a drunk, one was the same as the other; the body was bad. Paul would disagree.

First, God is for the body—an idea that appeals to me as I get older and fewer parts work and those that do work don't work like they used to. Saint Francis was right: "Brother Ass" is just the right name for one's body, often stubborn and always absurd. Yet Paul affirms that the Lord is for my body.

Second, the body is for the Lord. He not only loves it, but He has a purpose for it. Our bodies were made to contain the living God and make His invisible attributes known. Looks don't matter—tall, dark, and handsome;

short, shot, and shapeless—our bodies are beautiful when they make His beauty known.

Furthermore, He has an eternal purpose for our bodies; this isn't all there is. "By his power God raised the Lord from the dead, and he will raise us also" (1 Cor. 6:14). When our bodies are redeemed and perfected, they'll display His beauty forever. That's what bodies are everlastingly for.

Because our bodies have an eternal destiny, Paul maintains that we shouldn't misappropriate them now. They aren't made for self-indulgence and impurity. Sex is good, but illicit sex prostitutes our bodies. It's a sellout. He calls us to "flee from sexual immorality" (v. 18). As he puts it, "All other sins a man commits are outside his body, but he who sins sexually sins against his own body" (v. 18). Sex outside of marriage is uniquely a sin against the body because it violates the purpose for which the body was made. Bodies aren't meant to be indulged on whim; they have a nobler purpose. They're made to contain God and display Him forever.

There was a saying in Corinth: "Food for the stomach and the stomach for food" (v. 13), by which the Corinthians meant that nature demanded satisfaction. The stomach was made for food and food was made for the body. When Mac-attacked, therefore, indulge oneself! True, Paul agreed, the body was made for food and food for the body, but we mustn't extrapolate from that principle to another—that the body was made for sex and sex for the body. No, the body is more than its parts and is made for more than sex and self-indulgence. It's a sanctuary intended for God and meant to house Him—a place where He can be seen and known.

This leads Paul to his bottom line: "Therefore honor God [manifest his glory] with your body" (v. 20).

That's what bodies are for!

But, you say, why would He want *my* body? It's the source of almost everything that's wrong with me. It has a dirty mind; it's lazy and self-indulgent; it's been abused by drugs and booze and too much partying. It has a sexually transmitted disease. It's wasted and ruined!

And yet God still wants your body. It doesn't need to be tanned, toned, and terrific for Him. He asks that you bring it to Him with its attendant problems so He can make something good of it.

Most of us don't know what to do with our bodies. We have a love-hate relationship with them—alternately trashing and treasuring them. They'll never truly please us until we give them to God. He made our bodies and only He knows what they're for.

Give your body to Him, and He'll let you know how to use it. Given God's love for you and your body, it's the only reasonable thing to do.

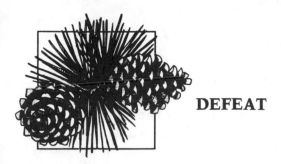

DEFEAT

Warm-up: Psalm 44

*For your sake we face
death all day long (Ps.
44:22).*

Most men want to be winners. We don't like to lose, especially when we lose big! We can all identify with Binkl Bogatej, the Yugoslavian ski jumper, whose spectacular miscue enlivens the introduction to ABC's "Wide World of Sports." He forever personifies the agony of defeat.

One of Israel's poets wrote about those times when all goes wrong. His poem, Psalm 44, helps me come to terms with my disasters. It strengthens me, puts starch into my spine. It's the place I often turn when I'm beat.

The author of Psalm 44 built the poem like a ziggurat, or stepped pyramid. Structurally, four tiers rise one above the other as the psalm advances to the last paragraph. At the foundation level the writer praised God for past victory (vv. 1–8); at the next level he lamented over present defeat (9–16); at the third he pled his innocence (17–22); and finally at the apex of the pyramid he prayed for deliverance (23–26).

Some date the psalm during the Exile, but others place it in Judah's heyday, when she was faithful to her cove-

nant, perhaps during the reign of one of her good kings—
Josiah, Jehoshaphat, or Hezekiah.

Judah's army had waged a holy war and suffered a shat-
tering defeat. Now the king leads the devastated, demoral-
ized army in prayer. Although the psalm was composed by
a member of the temple musician's guild, one of the Sons
of Korah, the poem appears to be written for the king.

The poet began by praising God for past victories: "We
have heard with our ears, O God; our fathers have told us
what you did in their days." What was done then, he
declared, was done "not by their sword . . . nor did their
arm bring them victory; it was your right hand, your arm,
and the light of your face, for you loved them" (vv. 1–3).
God was the secret of their success.

And the secret was not lost, he continued: "I do not
trust in my bow [either] . . . you give us victory over our
enemies." The king and his army could not be faulted.
They, like their predecessors, went out to do battle in
faith. But they met disaster; they were routed, slaughtered, scattered, disgraced, and humiliated (vv. 9–16).
"Where," in effect they asked, "did we go wrong? We
have not forgotten You nor been false to your covenant."
Furthermore, they said, "You know it's true because you
know the secrets of our hearts. Why have we been beaten
down?" (v. 21).

The answer comes at the point of greatest perplexity:
"Yet for your sake we face death all day long; we are
considered as sheep to be slaughtered (22)." This is the
crux of the psalm. The Israelites were suffering for God's
sake and not their own. Death and defeat was the price
they had to pay for their loyalty to him.

From the Exodus on the Israelites experienced the hos-
tility of demons and men simply because they were

God's people. The Israelites were caught up in the struggle of the kings of the earth against the Lord and His Messiah (Ps. 2). Their suffering was a sign of their fellowship with their Lord.

And thus we suffer because we are aligned with Him. "Everyone who wants to live a godly life in Christ Jesus will be persecuted" (2 Tim. 3:12). We too are linked with God in cosmic conflict with demons and men, and death and destruction is often the price we must pay for being in league with God. When we're attacked and when we lose out, we may be bewildered like the battered king of Psalm 44, but suffering comes not because we're in the wrong but because we're on the right side. In such instances we can be sure that we're still on the right course. As F. B. Meyer said, "If I'm told that I'm in for a hard journey, every hard jolt along the way reminds me that I'm on the right road."

The resolution of the poet's problem led him to prayer. "Rise up and help us; redeem us because of your unfailing love" (v. 26). God's love is the last word. Israel's defeat was only apparent; underneath stood God's loyalty and His everlasting love.

The apostle Paul well understood the message of Psalm 44. He assures us that nothing can separate us from the love of Christ, not "trouble or hardship or persecution or famine or nakedness or danger or sword" (Rom. 8:35). Then recalling Psalm 44, he declares, "*For your sake* we face death all day long, we are considered as sheep to be slaughtered" (italics mine). Despite impending slaughter, "in all these things, we are more than conquerors through him who loved us" (Rom. 8:37). Our defeats are only apparent; underneath resides everlasting love. When we fall, we fall into His arms.

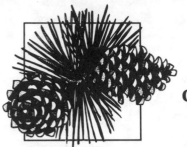

OBEDIENCE

He cried out to the man of God who had come from Judah, "This is what the LORD says: 'You have defied the word of the LORD and have not kept the command the LORD your God gave you'" (1 Kings 13:21).

Josephus, the Jewish historian, said his name was Jadon, but no one knows for sure. We only know him as the man of God who, "by the word of God came from Judah to Bethel" (v. 1). He came to announce judgment to Jeroboam, the king of Israel who had "put God behind him." The young prophet appeared at Jeroboam's altar at Bethel, made a promise that good King Josiah would profane Jeroboam's worship center (a prediction fulfilled about 300 year later), and sealed that promise with a sign. Jeroboam's altar disintegrated right in front of his eyes! Jadon was clearly a prophet—a man who had God's word.

Jeroboam tried to restrain the prophet, first by threat and then by bribe, but the young man of God was uncompromising. "Even if you were to give me half your possessions, I would not go with you, nor would I eat bread or drink water here. For I was commanded by the word of the LORD: 'You must not eat bread or drink water or return by the way you came.' So he took another road and did not return by the way he had come to Bethel" (13:8–10). Let's hear it for Jadon! No concession; no capitulation. He walked into Jeroboam's court and out again, unscathed, true to the truth.

But on the way home he encountered another prophet—a decaying old derelict, supported by Jeroboam's court and paid to keep his mouth shut—who had come out to entice him. "'Are you the man of God who came from Judah?' he asked. 'I am,' he replied. So the prophet said to him, 'Come home with me and eat.' The man of God said, 'I cannot turn back and go with you, nor can I eat bread or drink water with you in this place. I have been told by the word of the LORD: "You must not eat bread or drink water there or return by the way you came."' The old prophet answered, 'I too am a prophet, as you are. And an angel said to me by the word of the Lord: "Bring him back with you to your house so that he may eat bread and drink water."' (But he was lying to him.) So the man of God returned with him and ate and drank in his house" (vv. 14–19).

Later, at dinner, the word of the LORD did come to the old prophet, and he cried out to the man of God who had come from Judah, "This is what the LORD says, 'You have defied the word of the LORD and have not kept the command the LORD your God gave you'" (v. 21). The young man's doom was foretold.

That evening, as the prophet made his way home, a lion stalked and dispatched him; and when travelers found his carcass and the lion still standing over the kill, they reported the unnatural incident in the city. When the old prophet heard the story he spoke the truth once more: "It is the man of God who defied the word of the LORD. The LORD has given him over to the lion, which has mauled him and killed him, as the word of the LORD had warned him" (v. 26).

And so the old scoundrel, only occupied with his own well-being, buried the prophet from Bethel in his own tomb, with the proviso that others someday bury his bones with those of the man of God, for, he said, "The message he declared by the word of the LORD against the altar in Bethel and against all the shrines on the high places in the towns of Samaria will certainly come true" (v. 32). And it did. Josiah demolished Jeroboam's altar and high place and desecrated the tombs of his false prophet, "in accordance with the word of the LORD proclaimed by the man of God who foretold these things" (2 Kings 23:16). Josiah spared the bones of the prophet from Judah and those of the old man with him.

You can't help wondering why God was so severe with his young man. He was devoted. Was his deviation so bad? He was a man of God. He delivered the word. And then having done his job, wearied by the journey, hungry, thirsty, relaxing for a moment under a tree, he was overwhelmed by sudden seduction, and swept away. Surely God understood his frame.

And indeed he did. He brought him home to be with him. But on this occasion the stakes were too high for God to go soft on Jadon's disobedience. Jeroboam must know that God says what He means and means it! Judgment was pronounced and judgment could not be averted. The fate of the nation was at stake. If God had winked at the prophet's wrong doing, Jeroboam might not have known the enormity of his transgression and the severity with which it would be judged. No, God could not this time overlook his prophet's sin.

Jeroboam didn't hear. He became the prime biblical example of an idolatrous king. But *we* must hear. We must know that God says what he means and means it! What is written is written. Once decided, God doesn't modify His word. The old man came claiming a new revelation. An *angel* had updated God's word! It sounded likely; it looked real. Perhaps the old prophet had seen an angel. Satan does masquerade as an angel of light (2 Cor. 11:14). But as Paul so urgently wrote: "Even if we or an angel from heaven should preach a gospel other than the one we [the apostles] preached to you, let him be eternally condemned!" (Gal. 1:8).

We do not "run ahead," as John said, but rather go back and "continue in the teaching of Christ." For "whoever continues in the teaching [of Christ] has both the Father and the Son. If anyone comes to you and does not bring this teaching, do not . . . welcome him" (2 John 9–10).

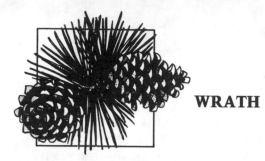

WRATH

His disciples remem-
bered that it is written:
"Zeal for your house will
consume me" (John
2:17).

There's another side to Jesus, the other side of Jesus, the one displayed at the Passover in Jerusalem. "In the temple courts he found men selling cattle, sheep and doves, and others sitting at tables exchanging money. So he made a whip out of cords, and drove all from the temple area, both sheep and cattle; he scattered the coins of the money changers and overturned their tables. To those who sold doves he said, 'Get these out of here! How dare you turn my Father's house into a market!'" (John 2:14–16).

Exchanging money and selling animals in the temple area wasn't wrong. Foreign pilgrims had to exchange their currency for Tyrian shekels. They couldn't easily bring sacrificial animals from long distances; it was more practical to purchase them in Jerusalem.

The wrong was in charging exorbitant exchange rates and selling animals for inflated prices. The clergy enriched themselves from religion. The temple was intended to be a place where people could draw near to

God. The clergy got in the way, and that made Jesus mad. That's the other side of Jesus, overturning tables, kicking stools, lashing people with His whip and with His tongue, putting the fear of God into them!

We see the rage of God in the face of Jesus—the incandescent wrath of the Lamb (Rev. 6:16).

His was legitimate outrage; the love of truth controlled Him. Zeal for the purity of His Father's house consumed Him (John 2:17). Our anger is rooted in impotence and frustration; His in righteousness. He cared enough about what was right to get very mad at wrong. That's why He tore things up in the temple.

We have a temple as well, or better said, we *are* a temple. Paul says that our bodies were made to be inhabited by God, designed to be the Father's house (1 Cor. 6:19–20). He'll enter any body. If you invite Him in, He'll make His home in you and make your heart a holy place (Rev. 3:20).

But He won't put up with clutter or anything that corrupts His house. If we too forget what our temples are for, be assured that He won't settle for it. He won't live with marital unfaithfulness, selfish ambition, greed, hatred, racism, an unforgiving heart, an evil indulgence, a subtle compromise, anything that defiles.

He'll woo us at first with his Word, appealing to us to resist evil. He's wonderfully patient with failure if we want to change; He slowly, relentlessly will rid us of all that defiles. His wrath is only for the hard and impenitent of heart (Rom. 2:5).

But if we parry His love, one day we'll look up to see Him standing there, His eyes ablaze, His whip in hand, turning the tables on us, upsetting our well-ordered lives, wreaking havoc. He will come to cast down, to deny, to rebuke, to interrupt. He will no longer be our friend, tolerant, understanding, patient. He will become for a time our enemy. His severity exposes our sin and drives it away. Though he may have to hurt us, he's ridding us of all that ultimately harms. He cares enough to be angry! That's the other side of Jesus.

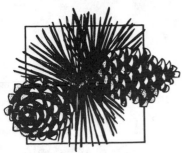

AFFLUENCE

Warm-up: Jeremiah 15:10–21

Blessed are you who are poor, for yours is the kingdom of God (Luke 6:20).

One of the more mournful aspects of modern Christianity is our insistent quest for an Unholy Grail. Early Christians would have abhorred our pursuit of ease and affluence. Back then no one would have believed that becoming a Christian could place a man among the rich and famous. Today for some it's considered a divine right. Some say that sickness, poverty, and infamy are signs of unbelief and that God wants us all to be healthy, wealthy, and wise. Apparently, then, the only victory that demonstrates closeness to God is full healing and circumstantial happiness. If only it were so.

Such a theology of success simply isn't so; God saves greater things for us than mere earthly happiness. Unscriptural and unrealistic expectations can plunge us into despair and unbelief and cause us to ignore what's really taking place.

According to Scripture, God has one great purpose in this world, which is to win back our hearts and make us one with Him. The entire Bible portrays God's love for humanity and His relentless seeking of those He loves.

65

In the pursuit of that purpose God may ask His own to do without for a while. Those aligned with God have not always had it easy. Suffering, crosses, scaffolds, prison, and pain have awaited them.

Jeremiah, that reluctant prophet, who was dragged into his job kicking and screaming, served God faithfully for nearly forty years. And for what? To be Judah's persona non grata, to be hounded and harassed. He was made for woe. He was flogged, battered, placed in stocks, nearly drowned in a cistern, dragged off to Egypt by his fellow exiles, and later, according to tradition, murdered by one of his own countrymen. Like the man who was tarred, feathered, and run out of town on a rail, were it not for the glory of the thing, Jeremiah would have passed it up.

But God never promised Jeremiah success; He only promised to deliver him in the midst of his trouble. God assured him: "I am with you to rescue and save you . . . I will save you from the hands of the wicked and redeem you from the grasp of the cruel" (Jer. 15:20–21).

The apostle Paul wrote from Rome's infamous Mamertine Dungeon: "At my first defense, no one came to my support, but everyone deserted me. . . . But the Lord stood at my side and gave me strength, so that through me the message might be fully proclaimed and all the Gentiles might hear it. And I was delivered from the lion's mouth. The Lord will rescue me from every evil attack and will bring me safely to his heavenly kingdom" (2 Tim. 4:16–17).

Shortly after Paul wrote those lines tradition says Nero's goons beheaded him on the Ostian Way. His deliverance was not physical but spiritual. He stood before Nero and gave a heroic and cogent defense of the Christian faith; he did not recant. His salvation was not from physical harm but from cowardice and capitulation—his own evil deeds.

God never promised us a gravy train, but He has promised to give us the real stuff of life when the going gets tough. He'll give us what we need to face whatever comes our way. His resources are available upon request. He does not promise to make us healthy or wealthy, but He will make us wise, banish bitterness, embellish our character, and use us to gather others to Himself.

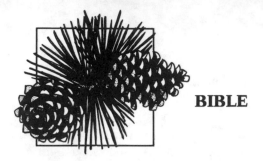

BIBLE

Warm-up: 2 Timothy 2:14–22

Present yourself to God as one approved, a workman who does not need to be ashamed and who correctly handles the word of truth (2 Tim. 2:15).

Most of us are biblically educated beyond our character, perhaps because we confuse the means with the end. We falsely assume that the purpose of Bible study is mere learning, a fallacy particularly characteristic of those of us who take the Bible straight.

But mere orthodoxy is never enough. Even the demons are orthodox (James 2:19). They study the Bible too. They make their own prophetic charts and draw their own theological lines, but the Book doesn't alter their behavior. They're devilish to the end.

In Paul's second letter to Timothy, he encouraged his young friend to be an approved workman "who does not need to be ashamed and who correctly handles the word of truth" (2 Tim. 2:15).

The word here translated "who correctly handles" means "one who goes for a goal." Classical Greek writers used the word of road builders who cut their way straight through a forest to a predetermined location. The Septuagint (the first Greek translation of the Old Testament) used the word in the last phrase of Proverbs 3:6: "In all your ways acknowledge him and he will make your paths straight [direct you to the goal]."

Paul contrasted good Bible study with the flawed methods of those who were "quarreling about words," which, he said, "is of no value, and only ruins those who listen" (2:14). Further, "godless chatter"—mere discussion of the Bible without the goal of godliness—will make one become "more and more ungodly" (2:16). Ironically, God's word, when misused, can make us less and less like God!

Paul therefore warns Timothy to "flee the evil desires of youth" (2:22), a command that in context has little or nothing to do with youthful *sexual* desires. Paul rather had in mind the wrong-headed passion of the young and the immature to argue about meaning—"word-fight" is the term he coins. Those who mishandle God's Word in this way are workmen who ought to be ashamed.

Instead of arguing about meaning, Timothy was to "pursue righteousness, faith, love and peace, along with those who call on the Lord out of a purified heart" (2:22). In other words, he was to seek God and his goodness through the Book. To do so is to handle the word correctly—to go straight to the goal.

The purpose of Bible study is clear. It ought to produce worship and make us more and more like our Lord. To the extent that we read the Scriptures for that reason our Bible reading is valid; to the extent that we do not, it's nonproductive. Worse, it's counterproductive, making us less and less like our Lord. Thus the hymnist prayed:

Beyond the sacred page, I seek Thee, Lord;
My spirit pants for Thee, O living Word.

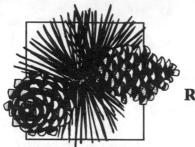

REPENTANCE

Warm-up: Genesis 4:1–15

*If you do what is right,
will you not be
accepted? But if you
do not do what is right,
sin is crouching at your
door; it desires to have
you, but you must
master it (Gen. 4:7).*

When Cain was born, Eve thought the promised seed had come: "I have gotten the God-man," she exclaimed.[1] But like all mothers, she was destined to be disappointed. Cain wasn't the Savior. He was just another sinner like his old man, a chip off the old block.

Cain and his brother Abel brought the fruit of their careers as an offering to the Lord. Cain offered *some* of his produce; Abel gave from the best of his flock. The offerings went on for a while but it was soon obvious to all that Cain's sacrifice was meaningless ritual. His heart wasn't in it (Heb. 11:4).

Cain was like many men I know who give lip service to the faith. They adorn their stationary with fish logos

---

[1]The Hebrew text reads, "I have gotten a man—the Lord."

and mouth the mottoes; but essentially they are looking out for themselves. Prestige and money are still their bottom line. They'll do almost anything to get ahead, a trifling devotion that's empty and unacceptable to God. God won't have unauthentic giving; He wants the whole man.

And what was Cain's response? Remorse? No. "Cain was very angry, and his face was downcast" (4:5). Half-hearted worship never gratifies. It only makes us more melancholy, which may be why there are so many frustrated, unhappy men around my town, full of latent anger and angst. No matter how many successes they accumulate, the bitterness and sadness will not go away.

But God always makes this appeal: "If you do what is right, will you not be accepted? But if you do not do what is right, sin [like a voracious beast] is crouching at the door; it desires to have you, but you must master it" (4:7).

No man is his own. We were made to be mastered. We'll either be God's subject or the slave of sin. There's no middle ground. We cannot have it both ways—outwardly offering ourselves to God, but inwardly worshiping at the altar of personal success. We *cannot* serve two masters. If we don't serve God with all our heart we'll go to any lengths to serve ourselves.

Cain refused to come to his senses and go to his knees. Hardening his heart he killed his brother (4:8–9), polluted his family and society with his ruthlessness (4:17ff.), and fled from God into the land of Nod (wandering), restless, lonely, and afraid. He would not face his sin.

It's odd how men pass the buck. No one wants to saddle himself with sin. Peters and Waterman call it a "fundamental attribution error." The successes in life are ours; the failures we attribute to others. I understand. I too have ingenious ways to avoid taking the rap for my wrong. But the guilt remains.

No matter how hard I try to run from my conscience I have a nagging conviction that I have gone wrong, and the guilt goes on.

We must stop fighting for our sin and start fighting against it. The way to begin is to face the fact of our failure. The Lord won't and can't heal anyone who minimizes his sin.

On the other hand, we must not minimize the grace of God. So much preaching these days only burdens others with guilt and does nothing to relieve it.

We must say that sin is sin. We must warn, but our "inevitable warnings must not be an end in themselves, but a reminder of the offer of grace held out by God" (Hans Kung). The gravity of our message must lead to the goodness of God. In the same breath with which we speak of sin we must proclaim the immensity of God's love for us and the totality of His forgiveness because of Christ's death for us. As Paul says, "God has reconciled [us] by Christ's physical body through death to present [us] holy in his sight, without blemish and free from all accusation" (Col. 1:22).

There's no other solution: there is no final forgiveness without repentance. As long as we waste time defending ourselves we'll get nothing done, and we'll never know the depths of God's love.

God put a mark on Cain to prolong his miserable life. He was waiting for Cain to come around. "He is patient . . . not wanting anyone to perish, but everyone to come to repentance" (2 Pet. 3:9). No one yet, not even Cain, has wandered too far to find the way back. We may take a hundred steps away from God, but it only takes one step to return. As long as we're alive, the promise is good: "If you do what is right will you not be accepted?" No one yet has out-sinned the grace of God.

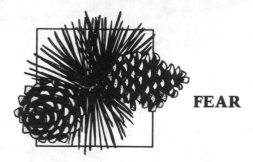

FEAR

*O our God, will you not
judge them? For we have
no power to face this
vast army that is
attacking us. We do not
know what to do, but
our eyes are upon you
(2 Chron. 20:12).*

King Jehoshaphat came down from his high in a hurry. After his good efforts to bring Judah back to God, "the Moabites and Ammonites with some of the Meunites came to make war on Jehoshaphat. Some men came and told Jehoshaphat, 'A vast army is coming against you from Edom, from the other side of the Sea. It is already in Hazazon Tamar' (that is, En Gedi)" (2 Chron. 20:1–2). En Gedi was only fifteen miles away, less than a day's march. The crisis was total!

Jehoshaphat was alarmed and sought the Lord, a reflex unknown to most of us ordinary men who first search our own minds for something to do. Jehoshaphat, an extraordinary man, stood with his people in the house of the Lord and girded up his loins with prayer.

Jehoshaphat focused first on God and found that everything was under control: "You rule over all the kingdoms of the nations [the hostile armies near-at-hand]. Power and might are in your hand, and no one can withstand you" (20:6). At ground level the view was appalling, but there was no panic above.

Then the king looked back and thought about God's faithfulness: "O our God, did you not drive out the inhabitants of this land before your people Israel and give it forever to the descendants of Abraham your friend?" (20:7).

God had given Canaan to Israel; no one could stop Him. And those alive when God gave it, who had learned their faith then, knew that when crises came a man could cry out to God and he would be heard and saved (20:9).

And so Jehoshaphat prayed: "Now here are men from Ammon, Moab and Mount Seir. . . . O our God, will you not judge them? For we have no power to face this vast army that is attacking us. We do not know what to do, but our eyes are on you" (20:10–12).

Then the Spirit of the Lord spoke through Jahaziel—one of the brothers: "Listen, King Jehoshaphat and all who live in Judah and Jerusalem! This is what the LORD says to you: 'Do not be afraid or discouraged because of this vast army. For the battle is not yours, but God's. Tomorrow march down against them. . . . You will not have to fight this battle. Take up your positions; stand firm and see the deliverance the LORD will give you. . . . Do not be afraid; do not be discouraged. Go out to face them tomorrow, and the LORD will be with you'" (20:15–18).

In the morning (which is when dread usually returns) Jehoshaphat reassured his people: "Listen to me. . . . Have faith in the LORD your God and you will be upheld; have faith in his prophets and you will be successful" (20:20). The band struck up a tune, and they went out together to face the foe, singing to one another an old sustaining song: "'Give thanks to the LORD, for his love endures forever.' As they began to sing and praise, the LORD set ambushes against the men of Ammon and Moab and Mount Seir who were invading Judah, and they were defeated. The men of Ammon and Moab rose up against the men from Mount Seir to destroy and anni-hilate them. After they finished slaughtering the men from Seir, they helped to destroy one another. When the men of Judah came to the place that overlooks the desert and looked toward the vast army, they saw only dead bodies lying on the ground; no one had escaped" (20:22–24).

There was nothing left of their foes but their bounty. "There was so much plunder that it took three days to collect it. On the fourth day they assembled in the Valley of Beracah, where they praised the LORD. This is why it is called the Valley of Beracah [blessing] to this day. Then, led by Jehoshaphat, all the men of Judah and Jeru-salem returned joyfully to Jerusalem, for the LORD had given them cause to rejoice over their enemies" (20:25–27).

We too have our adversaries—controlling people, com-pelling habits and moods—that take us by surprise. They come unbidden and unexpected, often after a life-changing decision or a period of spiritual gain. We should expect it. Every advance will be met by a counter-attack from the far side.

We must not focus on our foes and our fear. We should rather turn from them to seek God's face and the tranquil place where He dwells. There's no panic there. And from that quiet place we can sally forth to face what we fear, singing to ourselves about His love, thanking Him for a contest *already* won, believing that the battle is not ours but the Lord's.

And when we begin to praise Him, He will do the rest. He will deliver us from fear itself and surprise us with joy. The valley that we dread will become a Valley of Blessing forever.

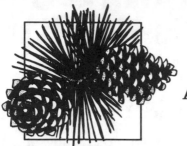

AVAILABILITY

Warm-up: Exodus 3:1–4:23

*So Moses thought, "I
will go over and see this
strange sight—why the
bush does not burn up"
(Exod. 3:3).*

Moses herded his father-in-law's flock on the backside of the desert for forty years of grinding, relentless duty. Once a part of Egypt's aristocracy—educated and finished in the best Egyptian schools, competent and adequate for anything—Moses now was nothing but a ragged goat-herder with no self-respect left. Once a man of strength and resolve, he had lost the desire to save even his own people. *Now* God could get to work.

One day near Sinai, where God made Himself known, Moses saw a bush ablaze and went off to investigate. Clearly this was no ordinary bush! Though it burned, it was not consumed. "I will go over," he said, "and see this strange sight" (3:3).

"When the LORD saw that he had gone over to look, God called to him from within the bush, 'Moses, Moses!' And Moses said, 'Here I am'" (3:4).

The mystery of the bush was explained by the presence of God; the meaning of the bush followed: "I have come down to rescue [my people] from the hand of the Egyptians and to bring them up . . . into a good and spacious land. . . . The cry of the Israelites has reached me, and I have seen the way the Egyptians are oppressing them. So now, go. I am sending you to Pharaoh to bring my people the Israelites out of Egypt" (3:8–10).

Forty years earlier Moses certainly would have taken on the task. Now he was full of disclaimer and doubt. Disappointment, failure, the loneliness of the desert, and the silence of God had broken his will. He asked, "Who am I, that I should go to Pharoah and bring the Israelites out of Egypt?" (3:11).

Moses had an identity crisis. He didn't know who he was. To establish Moses' worth God did not list his assets, talents, and abilities. Instead God informed Moses of His presence. "I will be with you," God said (3:12). Who we are doesn't matter. What matters is that God dwells *with* us, giving us the worth we need. Worth grows out of worship and walking with God, knowing we are loved and highly esteemed by Him.

Moses' second problem was ignorance. He didn't know who God was. "Suppose I go to the Israelites and say to them, 'The God of your fathers has sent me to you,' and they ask me, 'What is his name?' Then what shall I tell them?" (3:13). Put another way, "If it makes no difference who I am, then *who are you?*"

God always shows Himself to the man who is prepared to accept Him: "*I am* [is] who I am. . . . Say to the Israelites: 'I AM has sent me to you'" (3:14, italics mine). Put another way, "*I am* whatever you need!" God would be what Moses needed—his wisdom, righteousness, and sanctification.

Still Moses held back: "What if they [the elders of Israel] do not believe me or listen to me and say, 'The Lord did not appear to you'?" He hadn't appeared for four hundred years! Moses' question now is one of authority: "How can I win friends and influence others? Why should they count on my words? Who would listen to a loser like me?"

God responded by giving him three signs, all of which attested to Moses' ability to do things no mere man could do. They were the guarantees that God was with him to will and to work for his good pleasure and purpose. Moses' authority lay not in his training, background, experience, intelligence, or appearance. His resume didn't matter. His influence was explainable only in terms of God.

Moses' fear lingered: "O Lord, I have never been eloquent, neither in the past nor since you have spoken to your servant. I am slow of speech and tongue."[1] The LORD said to him, "Who gave man his mouth? Who makes him deaf or dumb? Who gives him sight or makes him blind? Is it not I, the LORD? Now go; I will help you speak and will teach you what to say" (4:10 -12).

Moses' problem now is inadequacy. We say: "I have no eloquence; God cannot use me!" But we must learn that God cares little for style or speech. What matters most is substance and spirit. As F. B. Meyer said, "God does not want excellency of speech or of language in his messengers, but the unction and power which come on those who speak after direct audience with the Eternal." If we have limitations—impediments, we say—they're not limitations to God. They are God-planned (Who made your mouth?) so that *He* can be strong.

---

[1] The language suggests that Moses had a serious speech impediment.

But Moses, still unpersuaded, carried on: "'O Lord, please send someone else to do it.' Then, the LORD's anger burned against Moses" (4:13–14). How odd of God to be outraged now. He tolerated Moses' deficiencies and doubts, but He fumed when Moses tried to pass the buck. In doing so, Moses expressed the only attitude that prevents God from putting a man to his intended use: lack of availability. God can handle inadequacy, but unavailability ties His hands.

We *are* inadequate. Therefore we should "confess ourselves poor creatures, for that is the beginning of being great men and great women. To try to persuade ourselves that we are something when we are nothing is a terrible loss; to confess that we are nothing is to lay the foundation of being something" (George MacDonald).

Deficiencies never disqualify. It's when we are weak that we are very strong.

One question remains: Why did God reveal Himself in a bush? Why settle for a shrub? The answer should be obvious: If available, any old bush will do!

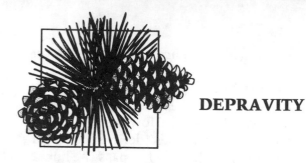

DEPRAVITY

*People will be lovers of
themselves . . . rather
than . . . God (2 Tim.
3:2–4).*

Something has gone wrong with us. As Paul said: "Men love themselves; they love money; they're proud, abusive, ungrateful, unholy, unloving, unforgiving, slanderous, without self-control, brutal; they don't love good; they're treacherous, rash, conceited, lovers of pleasure rather than lovers of God" (2 Tim. 3:24, paraphrase). We read the list and find ourselves there, somewhere.

Paul suggested a misdirected love: "Men love *themselves* rather than *God.*" We can't love others because we love ourselves too much. It's this crowning of self that leads to every other hurt, that jars other's hearts and makes them ache. We cause pain in ourselves and others because we're depraved. As Pogo said, "We have met the enemy and he is us!"

Aleksandr Solzhenitsyn learned about depravity as he pondered the meaning of his imprisonment in a Soviet gulag. "And it was only when I lay there on rotting prison straw that . . . it was disclosed to me that the line separating good from evil passes not through states, nor between classes, nor between parties either—but right through every human heart, through all human hearts."

Theologians have two terms for our sinfulness. They talk about original sin and total depravity. Original sin doesn't mean that we sin in very original ways. Most of us sin like everyone else. Original sin means that we're sinful in our origins. We come into the world with a proclivity for doing wrong. We're like a baseball with a spin on it; sooner or later we break and the break is down and out. Total depravity means that sin touches the totality of our being. If sin were a color, we would be some shade of sin all over.

Unctuous preachers didn't contrive the word *sinner* to shake us up (or shake us down) on Sunday mornings; it's a painful reality, manifested in individual acts of our own making. The miserable thing is that there's evil in our being that does not care for God, makes us desire wrong, and causes us to act badly. We sin because we're sinful, and worst of all, we like it!

You can't do much about evil in others; there's really only one person anyone can do very much about. As George MacDonald said, "Foolish is the man, and there are many such men, who would rid himself or his fellows of discomfort by setting the world right, by waging war on the evils around him, while he neglects that integral part of the world where lies his business, his first business—namely his own character and conduct."

It's our own indwelling badness, ready to produce evil, that makes life hard for others. But when we see what we are and turn against evil, at that same moment evil begins to die. We are then on the Lord's side, as He has always been on ours, and He begins to deliver us from who we are. He came to free us from sin that dwells and works in us. And He gives not only freedom from the evil things we've done, but the possibility of not doing them any more.

We don't have to go on hurting the ones we love. We can heal others by helping ourselves. When one man repents and is made right, it's the beginning of the cure of the whole world.

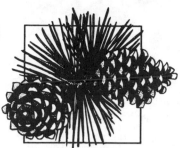

PRODIGAL

Warm-up: Luke 15:11–32

*"This son of mine was
dead and is alive again;
he was lost and is
found." So they began to
celebrate (Luke 15:24).*

A certain young man had a father who gave him a warm and safe home, food to eat, and most of all his love and loyalty. The young man could have lived happily ever after, but he didn't like the house rules. He wanted to be on his own.

The father thought otherwise; he knew a young man needed limits and respect for boundaries. His son would only be at odds with himself, utterly unhappy with a freedom that knew no fear, limits, or respect for others.

But the boy wanted to leap the fences. Life's mysteries beckoned; his pulse raced; he feared he might miss out on life. He must find himself; as we say, he had to have space.

His friends agreed. It's good, they said, for a man to assert himself. You have to risk the boy to find the man. There comes a time to be recognized, to get yourself free.

The boy demanded his inheritance. After all, he argued, it's mine; I have it coming to me. So the father gave him his legacy. Now he could do as he pleased, never stopping to think that all he possessed came from his father. He wasn't thankful for his father's love.

He couldn't stay in his hometown—too many reminders of his father's presence—so, like Kipling, he looked for a place "where there ain't no Ten Commandments." He hied himself to San Francisco where a man can quickly find and lose himself. He bought a condo by the bay, a new wardrobe, an SL450. He was an instant sensation, one of the beautiful people.

He spent lavishly and threw himself into the company of trendy friends, but something was amiss. A persistent melancholy hounded him, a dreary sameness, a monotony that he could not shake. The more unhappy he became, the more he diverted himself by celebrating. And then he realized his diversions controlled him. He could no longer be alone or free.

Most of his friends shared the same fate. They had that hollow look in their eyes; their faces told their story. He saw the "marks of weakness, marks of woe."

He went from bad to worse—a downturn that drove him to the sinks of skidrow. He ran out of money and friends. Left with nothing but unsatisfied longing, he turned to drugs to ease the pain. Freedom became "just another word for nothing left to lose." He had neither morality nor modesty.

Then one day he awoke to remember his father's house and its joy. He remembered the good things: the love, the warmth, the knowledge that he belonged. He knew then he was homesick; he had to go home.

But not as a son; he had forfeited his right to be called his father's son. He would go and ask for a mere servant's role, anything to get back home. And so he packed a bag and caught a bus for home. On the way he rehearsed his lines: "Father, I have sinned against heaven and against you. I am no longer worthy to be your son; make me like one of your hired men."

When he was only a speck in the distance, his father saw him. He ran as fast as his tottering, old legs could carry him, threw his arms around his son, and kissed him. He brought him to the house and gave him new clothes and shoes. Then he threw a barbecue for all the neighbors, and he told every guest, "This son of mine was dead, but now he's alive again."

Jesus told this story of the prodigal son over two thousand years ago, but the picture of the waiting Father has not faded. Our heavenly Father still loves us and waits patiently and longingly for us to come home.

In one way or another, we are all like the wayward son. We have our dark ages. We fool around with sex, drugs, ambition, and a hundred other diversions. He permits us to use our bodies for self-gratification, our energy to pursue selfish ends, and even our minds to devise arguments against Him. And He will let us search restlessly, relentlessly until we utterly weary ourselves. When we exhaust our options, we turn to Him. Before we can even ask for help, He wraps us in His arms and will not let us go. As T. S. Eliot wrote:

> And we shall not cease from exploration
> And the end of all our exploring
> Will be to arrive where we started,
> And know the place for the first time.

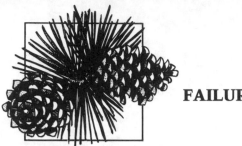

FAILURE

If anybody does sin, we have one who speaks to the Father (1 John 2:1).

Only a few baseball players have ever batted .400 over an entire season, which means they went hitless six out of ten times. Somehow that makes me feel better about myself.

We focus too much on success stories; Christians, like the champions of Homeric epics, always make it big. I confess I get tired of hearing such heroics. Emerson was right: "Every hero gets to be a bore at last." Personally, I'd like to hear a few more stories about failures like me.

Fortunately, the Bible is full of them: Noah drank too much, Abraham lied, Moses lost his temper, Gideon lost his nerve, Peter kept putting both feet in his mouth, Paul was sometimes curt and inconsiderate, Mark went home to mother, and Thomas doubted. Most biblical men and women cut unheroic figures, but they're still my heroes. I need some failures to look up to now and then.

David is my favorite; he muffed it so many times. And yet the Bible described him as a man after God's own heart. How can it be? Is there hope for a sinner like me? It seems there is; it all depends on the state of the heart.

David is best known for his affair with Uriah's pretty little wife, Bathsheba, whom he saw exposed on her patio. One wrong thing led to another. As Augustine would say, "Her caresses drew his spirit down." Bathsheba got pregnant. David let a contract on her husband, an old friend, and after his death, married her to put a legal and final end to the sordid affair, or so he thought.

The law of inevitable consequence caught up with the king. He had to face the facts; or, more precisely, he had to face Nathan, who dug up the facts. The prophet trapped David with a trumped-up story about a rich man who stole another man's lamb to serve a "traveling stranger," Nathan's metaphor for David's transient passion.

When David heard the story he was outraged. "As surely as the LORD lives, the man who did this deserves to die!" David, of course, overreacted; sheep-nabbing was not a capital crime. Or perhaps he knew what Nathan was really talking about. When David realized that Nathan had his number, his defenses crumbled. "I have sinned against the LORD," he said (2 Sam. 12:13). David didn't cover up; he faced his failure and repented of it and the Lord took away his sin. David bore the serious consequences of his sin, but his walk with God resumed. He could go on.

Some of David's most poignant and powerful poems were composed during this period (Psalms 32, 38, and 51). They reveal the state of his heart.

I acknowledged my sin to you
and did not cover up my iniquity.
I said, "I will confess
my transgressions to the LORD"—

and you forgave
the guilt of my sin.
Therefore let everyone who is godly pray to you
while you may be found (Psalm 32:5–6).

The word *godly* may put us off because we may think
of someone who is sinless. The original word merely sig-
nified one who was loyal to the Lord and longed to please
Him.

Anyone can be godly because what matters most is not
performance but the inclination of the heart. As Jesus
said, "Blessed are those who hunger and thirst for righteousness, for they will be filled" (Matt. 5:6).

God doesn't look for perfection; He knows the miserable stuff of which we're made. The godly will surely sin
and just as certainly their sins will be found out. God
reveals our waywardness to heal us. We will notice defilement because He will show it to us; such work in us
is the sign of His presence. And when that sin is faced
and repented of, it is forgiven. Then we can go on. And
going on, after all, is what matters. God doesn't require
perfection, only progress.

C. S. Lewis wrote, "No amount of falls will really undo
us if we keep picking ourselves up each time. We shall of
course be very muddy and tattered children by the time
we reach home . . . The only fatal thing is to lose one's
temper and give up."

COMPASSION

Warm-up: Psalm 103

*He does not treat us as
our sins deserve (Ps.
103:10).*

You may recall *Playing for Time,* the movie about Fanla
Fénelon, who was in an orchestra composed of Jewish
women who were spared the gas chambers at Auschwitz
as long as they played well. Their lives were reduced to a
single proposition: do well or die.

I sometimes feel like Fanla, thinking God has given me
a very difficult instrument to play and is watching every
move, listening to every sound, waiting for me to hit
some sour notes. My life is reduced to a single proposition: do well or die. But it isn't so! Despite the miscues
and the dissonant chords in my life, the untuned and
untunable nature of it, Jesus loves me. This I know, for
the Bible tells me so. "The LORD is compassionate and
gracious, slow to anger, abounding in love. He will not
always accuse, nor will he harbor his anger forever; he
does not treat us as our sins deserve or repay us according
to our iniquities" (Ps. 103:8–10).

Despite our intentions to live right, we've failed; we've
gone very wrong. We may believe that God can't love the
likes of us. But He does. He suffers fools gladly; He has
compassion on those who fear Him.

The Strength of a Man

Beyond our determination and earnestness solidly lies God's persistence. Theologs speak of the perseverence of man, but what of God's perseverance—His pulling, prodding, calling, wooing? We may have given up on Him, but He's not going to give up on us.

Even if we're on the run—trying to get away from Him—He's in pursuit. Those footsteps behind us are His; He's gaining on us. Though we take flight, He'll pursue us with His love. He's the "Hound of Heaven" as Francis Thompson said:

> I fled him down the nights and down the days;
> I fled him down the arches of the years;
> I fled him down the labyrinthine ways;
> Of my own mind; and in the midst of tears
> I hid from him, and under running laughter.
> Up vistaed slopes I sped, and shot precipitated
> Down titanic gloom of chasmed fears,
> From those strong feet that followed, followed
>   after. . . .

He stays with us to the end. He's not put off by false starts or sour notes. He is the God of the hard case, the difficult temperament, the unfit and the misfit. He'll not give up until He sees His character formed in us. No failure is final; He's the God of another chance.

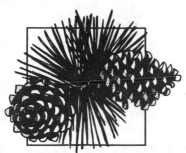

WORLDLINESS

Warm-up: Matthew 5:17–48

*Do not love the world or
anything in the world
(1 John 2:15).*

When I was a young man, people who talked about world-liness puzzled me. I knew the world ought to be avoided; the Bible said, "Love not the world." But for the good of me, I could not pin the idea down. What was worldliness? No one seemed to know for sure. At least no all-inclusive list of vices existed that could be identified as worldly. For some, it was smoking and drinking; for others it was card playing, gambling, and moviegoing. Once at a church camp they cautioned us that mixed bathing (swimming) was worldly, although I wasn't at all sure with what I should not be mixed. I learned later it was girls.

Few people could adequately explain why these activities were wrong. At least their explanations never really satisfied me. I was told that smoking defiled my body, which was God's temple; but those who so defined world-liness ate junk food and defiled their bodies through over-work and sedentary life-styles.

Furthermore, I noted that you could avoid bars and beer busts and still harbor bitterness, jealousy, and petty attitudes that even my non-Christian friends tried to avoid. I saw nonsmokers who were ruthless in their pursuit of money, who exploited and ran roughshod over others to enrich themselves, and who were infamous in the business community for their lack of integrity. Yet, these were the men frequently asked to become the elders in the local church because they had made it big as Christian businessmen. I observed church-going women who never missed a prayer meeting or Bible study yet gossiped and spread rumors. And significantly, they were the most miserable women I knew. And then I noticed certain clergy who preached against worldliness but wanted to be pampered and pandered to, and who became angry and defensive when their authority was challenged. It didn't add up.

Now don't get me wrong. I can think of plenty of reasons for avoiding some activities. Smoking impairs one's health. The Surgeon General has established a link between lung cancer and smoking; anyone who reads cigarette packs knows that's so. It doesn't make much sense to smoke if it's so obviously harmful to one's body. And for various reasons people go on the wagon. Some men I know have decided to abstain or become more moderate drinkers in view of the rising crime and accident rate from increased alcohol consumption. There are commonsense reasons for avoiding or curtailing drinking and smoking—reasons both religious and nonreligious people can agree on.

But to use these conventions and taboos as indicators of character misses the point. The Bible defines worldliness by centering morality where we intuitively know it should be. Worldliness is the lust of the flesh (a passion for sensual satisfaction), the lust of the eyes (an inordinate desire for the finer things of life), and the pride of life (self-satisfaction in who we are, what we have, and what we have done).

Worldliness, then, is a preoccupation with ease and affluence. It elevates creature comfort to the point of idolatry; large salaries and comfortable life-styles become necessities of life. Worldliness is reading magazines about people who live hedonistic lives and spend too much money on themselves and wanting to be like them. But more importantly, worldliness is simply pride and selfishness in disguise. It's being resentful when someone snubs us or patronizes us or shows off. It means smarting under every slight, challenging every word spoken against us, cringing when another is preferred before us. Worldliness is harboring grudges, nursing grievances, and wallowing in self-pity. These are the ways in which we are most like the world.

Jesus asserted that justice, mercy, and faithfulness are the weightier matters of the Law (Matt. 23:23). Christian morality centers itself in personal righteousness, not in mere abstinence from strong drink and tobacco and other externals. We ought to be like Jesus, full of grace and truth. It's in this way that we are most unlike the world.

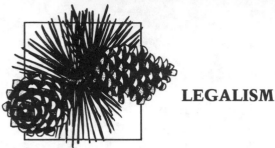

LEGALISM

*These people honor me
with their lips, but their
hearts are far from me.
Their worship of me is
made up of only rules
taught by men (Isa.
29:13).*

The clergy saw some of Jesus' men eating without washing their hands and confronted Him: "Why don't your disciples live according to the tradition of the elders instead of eating their food with 'unclean' hands?" (Mark 7:5). The question had nothing to do with hygiene. It was a matter of convention, rules and regulations to clean up one's act with God. It was legalism, an effort to generate righteousness by rules.

"Hypocrites!" Jesus barked. "Isaiah was right: Your worship is empty; your hearts have gone wrong; you've made your own rules and foisted them on men!"

The word *hypocrite* seems harsh unless we understand its meaning. A hypocrite is a person who's outwardly correct and inwardly corrupt. The clerics taught decency but their hearts were defiled. Their rules could neither correct the state of their own hearts nor could they correct others.

Later on Jesus admonished the crowd: "Listen to me everyone, and understand this. Nothing outside a man can make him 'unclean' by going into him. Rather, it is what comes out of a man that makes him 'unclean'" (v. 14).

When the disciples asked for another explanation He replied: "Don't you see that nothing that enters a man from the *outside* can make him 'unclean'? . . . What comes out of a man is what makes him 'unclean.' For from *within*, out of men's hearts, come evil thoughts, sexual immorality, theft, murder, adultery, greed, malice, deceit, lewdness, envy, slander, arrogance and folly. All these evils come from *inside* and make a man 'unclean'" (vv. 18–23, italics mine).

The problem with sin is that it's *within*. Nothing external can cure it. Edicts, dictums, and decrees may "indeed have an appearance of wisdom," but as Paul said, "they lack any value in restraining sensual indulgence" (Col. 2:23). Rules don't work; they won't change us. They can only make things worse.

And yet people keep telling us that tradition, rite, or ritual will modify us. But they fail us. Even our disciplines do. In our determination to right some wrong within, we may read the Bible more, pray more, memorize more Scripture, and go to church more often; but these activities, though good, can't change us. They can only draw us closer to the One who can.

The way to handle sin is to give it to God. No law or custom can make us new. We can't horn in on His work. The way to change is to ask Him to change us by His own working—from within.

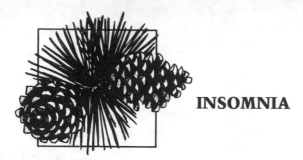

INSOMNIA

Warm-up: Psalm 77

*I will remember the
deeds of the LORD (Ps.
77:11).*

There are those seemingly interminable nights when we awaken and can't make our way out of the muddle. We remember all the things gone wrong—unmet duties, unpaid debts, and undeserved criticism. In the middle of the night, marketing techniques and management insights won't do.

Underlying our disquiet are the questions: Has God given up on me? Will He ever show His face again? Does He love me? Has He discarded me because of my sin?

But to ask the questions is to answer them; He cannot impugn His own character. Even if "we are faithless, he will remain faithful, for he cannot disown himself" (2 Tim. 2:13). We've forgotten the character of God.

But we remember again, older memories, older than our failures and others': "To this I will appeal: the years of the right hand of the Most High" (Ps. 77:10). Or to put it another way, we recall the good old days when the Most High rolled up His sleeves. We think back and, like the psalmist, we remember: "Your *ways*, O God, are holy. What god is so great like our God?" (v. 13, italics mine).

God's ways are not the ways of men and other gods;
His ways are holy; they are unique. He once made a way
through the sea.

> The waters saw you, O God,
> the waters saw you and writhed;
> the very depths were convulsed.
>
> The clouds poured down water,
> the skies resounded with thunder;
> your arrows flashed back and forth.
>
> Your thunder was heard in the whirlwind,
> your lightning lit up the world;
> the earth trembled and quaked.
>
> Your path led through the sea,
> your way through the mighty waters,
> though your footprints were not seen.
>
> You led your people like a flock
> by the hand of Moses and Aaron (16–20).

A way through the sea? Poetic license? Semitic hy-
perbole? No. When God's people had their backs
against the wall, He led them like a flock through mighty
waters. He opened a way through the Red Sea, even
though as the poet observed, "his footprints were not
seen" (v. 19).

That's the thing about God; we can't always see His
footprints! He goes where no one has ever gone before.
He does the unexpected, the unanticipated, the unfore-
seen. He delivers in unprecedented ways. And somehow,
someway, He'll make a way for us through the sea. Some
nights we forget to remember!

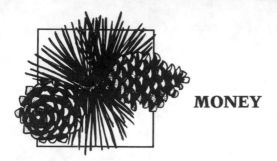

MONEY

Warm-up: 1 Timothy 6:6–19

Where your treasure is,
there your heart will be
also (Matt. 6:21).

Jesus warned against storing up treasure for ourselves here on earth because moth and rust can destroy it and thieves can steal it. We should send our treasure on to heaven where nothing rusts and no one can rip us off. The truly gilt-edged security is on ahead.

Our Lord wasn't banning possessions nor saying we shouldn't save for a rainy day. Storing up and being stewardly is necessary and therefore good (cf. Prov. 12:27; 13:4, 22). His concern is more with wisdom in our investments.

Money doesn't last very long. "Easy come; easy go" is at least half right, which is why Paul says we shouldn't put our hope in *uncertain* riches (1 Tim. 6:17, italics mine).

Because money goes, we can't enjoy it for fear of losing it. We try to shelter it, but someone is always ready to take it away from us. Someone once pointed out to me that foolproof schemes rarely work. Fools are too ingenious.

And if our money doesn't go, then sooner or later we do, and we can't take it with us. Our sure demise is like that of the stockbroker who encountered a genie on the way to the office and when given a wish asked for a copy of his local newspaper one year hence. He hurriedly turned to the market page to plan his killing in stocks, but he got more than he bargained for. On the opposite page, he spied his picture in an obituary, describing his death in an automobile accident.

But Jesus' concern for our money runs far deeper than the danger of losing it all in the end. He's more interested in what it does to our hearts right now. Loving money affects our hearts by impairing our ability to "see." As Jesus put it in His enigmatic way, "If your eyes are good, your whole body will be full of light. But if your eyes are bad, your whole body will be full of darkness" (Matt. 6:22–23). If we gaze at money and want it badly enough, our hearts will go bad.

The love of money draws our hearts away from *good*. We become confused and uncertain; our judgment is clouded and we begin to make bad decisions, ones that defy logic and deny our own values. As Paul warned us, "People who want to get rich fall into temptation and a trap and into many foolish and harmful desires that plunge men into ruin and destruction. For the love of money is a root of all kinds of evil" (1 Tim. 6:9–10). When you love money, you'll go to almost any lengths to get it. When the light within has gone out, how great is the darkness (cf. Matt. 6:23).

Ultimately, money draws our hearts away from *God*. As Jesus said, "No one can serve two masters. Either he will hate the one and love the other, or he will be devoted to the one and despise the other. You cannot serve both God and Money" (Matt. 6:24).

Jesus doesn't condemn materialism because it deprives the poor but because it deprives us. We lose our vision of

God. We cannot serve two masters. We can have only one center at a time. If money fascinates us, we will lose our fascination with Him.

How can we rid ourselves of our affection for things other than God and our preoccupation with them? Devotion to Him, worship of Him, service for Him—what Jesus called storing up treasure in heaven—are what loosen our grip on lesser things and set our affection on things above. Worshiping money limits our love for God; worshiping Him loosens money's grip upon us.

The bottom line of all investment is return. What do we get for our effort? If we invest solely in things on the earth, we'll lose them all. But if we invest ourselves in knowing God and in loving Him, it's an investment that's truly secure.

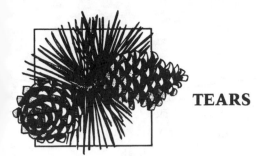

TEARS

Warm-up: 2 Corinthians 4:7–18

*Our light and
momentary troubles are
achieving for us an
eternal glory that far
outweighs them all
(2 Cor. 4:17).*

My little granddaughter sat on my lap the other day and sobbed. I can't recall now what made her cry—some trifling thing. But it wasn't trivial to her. She wept as though her heart would break. Her tears touched me and kindled my own small pain, and I thought of the words of George Matheson's wonderful old hymn:

O Joy that seekest me through pain,
I cannot close my heart to thee,
I trace the rainbow through the rain,
And feel the promise is not vain
That morn shall tearless be.

Matheson was thinking of the promised new world where God will once more dwell with people, where the Sun of Righteousness will rise and there will be no more darkness. "He will wipe every tear from their eyes. There will be no more death, or mourning, crying or pain" (Rev. 21:4). Then God will wipe every tear from our eyes. Heaven is the joy that seeks us through our pain—the final answer to our tears.

It's an old answer. Long ago it was rumored that one day our sorrow would be turned into joy. "On this mountain [Zion]" . . . as Isaiah said, "[God] will swallow up death forever. The Sovereign LORD will wipe away the tears from all faces" (Isa. 25:7–8).

Scripture habitually contrasts our tears with the joys of heaven. Paul considered our present sufferings not worth comparing with the glory to be revealed (Rom. 8:18). He believed "our light and momentary troubles are achieving for us an eternal glory that far outweighs them all" (2 Cor. 4:17). That's why, he said, he fixed his eye "not on what is seen, but on what is unseen. For what is seen is temporary, but what is unseen is eternal" (v. 18).

We don't fix our eyes much on heaven these days. Perhaps it seems unearthly, too much like "pie in the sky by-and-by." Some have suggested that we ought to get on with the business of earth and that "heavenly-minded people are no earthly good."

There are many things yet to be done right here, but as C.S. Lewis wrote, "either there is pie in the sky or there is not. If there is not, then Christianity is false, for this doctrine is woven into its whole fabric. If there is, then this truth, like any other, must be faced whether it be useful in political meetings or not."

Christianity clearly says that heaven is the ultimate answer to the problem of pain. Any solution that fails to put the joys of heaven over against the tears of earth cannot be called a Christian solution. To be thoroughly Christian is to believe that this earth is not all there is. There's a new day breaking, a "unique day," to quote the prophet (Zech. 14:7), when our Lord will come to take away our sorrow and wipe away our tears.

Christians aren't stoics; they cry. Our dreams and our hearts get broken. We grieve but we do not "grieve like the rest of men, who have no hope" (1 Thess. 4:13). We "trace the rainbow through the rain, and feel the promise is not vain that morn shall tearless be."

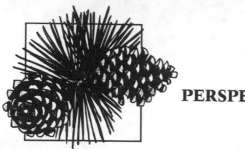

PERSPECTIVE

Warm-up: Genesis 13

*All the land that you see
I will give to you and
your offspring forever
(Gen. 13:14).*

Consider Abraham's way of looking at things. He saw the difference between what is permanent and what is merely passing. It's a matter of perspective.

Abraham and his nephew Lot got into conflict over a piece of land. It's an old story. Abraham became wealthy in Egypt, and God blessed him despite his sin. Perhaps that's when Abraham began to learn grace; He got what he didn't deserve.

Lot was also enriched in Egypt and as a result, "The land could not support them while they stayed together, for their possessions were so great that they were not able to stay together. And quarreling arose between Abram's herdsmen and the herdsmen of Lot. The Canaanites and Perizzites were also living in the land at that time" (Gen. 13:6–7). Someone had to give.

Abraham normally wasn't passive; he was a fighter. Yet on this occasion, he yielded to a younger, lesser man. "Let's not have any quarreling between you and me or between your herdsmen and mine, for we are brothers. Is not the whole land before you? Let's part company. If you go to the left, I'll go to the right; if you go to the right, I'll go to the left" (Gen. 13:8–9).

Abraham could have insisted on his rights; God had given the land to him, but there was more at stake than mere land. The Canaanites were looking on. Anyway, the earth didn't mean that much to him; he foresaw a "better country—a heavenly one" (Heb. 11:16). Therefore, he could give ground; he could let Lot choose.

Abraham chose grace; Lot chose grass. He saw the irrigated plains of the Jordan, where the Sodomites were and the people of Gomorrah, and he settled there in their cities (Gen. 13:10). Eventually he lost everything—his family, his prosperity, his integrity. The city corrupted him. He was almost swept away in the judgment on Sodom.

"The Lord said to Abram after Lot had parted from him, 'Lift up your eyes from where you are and look north and south, east and west. All the land that you see I will give to you and your offspring forever . . . Go, walk through the length and breadth of the land, for I am giving it to you'" (13:14–17).

Lot chose land and lost everything; Abraham let God choose and got everything forever. He fixed his eyes "not on what is seen, but on what is unseen. For what is seen is temporary, but what is unseen is eternal" (2 Cor. 4:18). He saw the difference between the permanent and the merely passing.

One of J. I. Packer's colleagues was denied tenure at a European university because of his faith, but when Packer commiserated with him, he replied, "Ah, but you see it doesn't matter. I have known God and they haven't."

My friend, Bob Young, was denied a doctorate from another university because his world view included

Jesus. He sang as he walked out the door, "I'd rather have Jesus than silver or gold. I'd rather have Jesus than riches untold. I'd rather have Jesus than anything this world affords to me."

It's a matter of perspective.

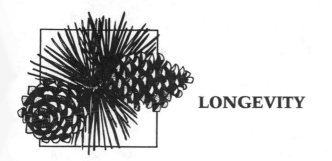

LONGEVITY

Warm-up: Mark 10:35–45

*The Son of Man did not
come to be served, but
to serve (Mark 10:45).*

A friend of mine used to ranch in the high desert south of
our place. Once when we were visiting his old homestead
he pointed out a gnarled juniper tree, the only one in
sight. You wouldn't travel far to see it and it isn't much
to look at, but it was doing its job—providing shade for a
cow or two. It's the best illustration I've ever seen of the
principle of blooming where you're planted.

His analogy made me think of another rancher I used
to know who lived near Lometa, Texas. His two grand-
sons were my best friends and we used to hunt doves on
his place. I've long since forgotten the hunting—most of
my hunting is forgettable—but I'll never forget the man.
He was someone special.

We used to go into town with him and follow him
around while he shopped and chatted with town folks
that he knew. He'd call them by name and he seemed to
know most of their needs. He'd stop here and there and
ask about a sick child or an ailing marriage, and then he'd
offer a word of encouragement, share a word of Scripture,
and pray if it seemed the thing to do. He didn't foist his
faith on anyone, but he always seemed to leave it behind.

He was a tough old fellow, but he had about him what Paul would call the sweet "aroma of Christ" (2 Cor. 2:15). He's gone to be with the Lord now, but his fragrance lingers on in Lometa.

Our fragrance can be long lasting if we stay put in one place, quietly manifesting Jesus' love, patiently tending His sheep and being faithful to the task no matter how long it takes or how much it costs. Even if no one else sees us or knows about us, God sees and knows and we're very big in His eyes.

We all get an occasional yen to move on to bigger things. Bigger is somehow better in our minds, although it shouldn't be. In God's eyes, there are no little places or little people. God's will isn't always upwardly mobile, and a call to something bigger isn't necessarily better and it isn't necessarily a call from Him.

God's will may be to move on, but I don't think we should move up just for ourselves. A career move merely to better one's self is surely not God's will. "Should you then seek great things for yourself?" Jeremiah asked. "Seek them not!" (Jer. 45:5). Prominence may come, but God should pass out the honors. Places of honor "belong to those for whom they have been prepared" (Mark 10:40). In the meantime we should grow and flourish right where we're planted until God Himself uproots us or to use Francis Schaeffer's colorful expression, until He "extrudes" us from our place. As the poet put it:

"Father, where shall I work today?"
And my love flowed warm and free.
He pointed out a tiny spot and said,
"Tend that place for me."

I answered him quickly, "Oh, no! Not that!
Why, no one would ever see,
No matter how well my work was done;
not that little place for me!"

The word he spoke, then, wasn't stern;
he answered me tenderly:
"Nazareth was a little place,
and so was Galilee."

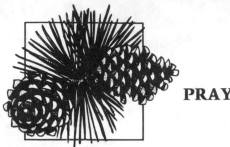

PRAYER

Warm-up: John 5:19–30

*One day Jesus was
praying in a certain
place. When he finished,
one of his disciples said
to him, "Lord, teach us
to pray, just as John
taught his disciples"
(Luke 11:1).*

Jesus baffles us as he baffled others. We see him hard at work—confronting the powers of demons and men and defeating them, vindicating widows and orphans, directed by an unknown source of strength and wisdom. We watch and wonder: Where did He get His authority?

One of Jesus' disciples overheard Him pray and determined that Jesus' remarkable powers were related to prayer. Certainly this disciple, as everyone does, prayed now and then when the chips were down. Even the impious pray. But he wanted something more and so cried out, "Lord teach us to pray!"

The Lord's prayer follows, the prayer we've been taught to follow in form. But the Prayer is more than ritual; it's rather a revelation of the *meaning* of prayer. When Jesus called God, "Father," he was expressing our utter dependence on Him.

112

Jesus followed no form in His prayers. On those occasions when we hear Him pray, such as in John 17, His prayers are informal. But if we listen, we will learn His secret; He prayed out of dependence. Perhaps the most startling of all Jesus' statements about Himself was his insistence that He too was a dependent being. Having laid aside the independent use of His deity, He declared, "By myself I can do nothing" (John 5:30).

And so He prayed without ceasing. Prayer was the environment in which He lived, the air He breathed. Subject to continual interruptions, busy beyond comparison, resisted by friends and foes, hassled and harried, He managed to keep in touch with God. Every situation was an occasion for prayer. When He held the small supply of bread and saw the multitude to be fed, He gave thanks first for God's supply. When He called Lazarus from the tomb, He called first on the Father. When the Greeks came seeking Him, knowing He had to come through, He asked God to glorify His name. Prayer was His principle work and by this He carried on the rest.

His life was continuous prayer. No demands, only dependence; no clamoring for attention, only a quiet continual reliance on the Father who always heard Him (John 11:42).

Saints of the middle ages saw in *everything* a summons to prayer: a church bell, the flight of a swallow, a sunrise, the falling of a leaf. Our vision of ourselves as needy, dependent men makes life a matter of continuous prayer, so much a part of us that we can say with the psalmist, "I am a man of prayer!" (Ps. 109:4).

And so the quintessence of life is prayer, not to demand but to wait with patience and submission, to long for and expect. By it everything else is done.

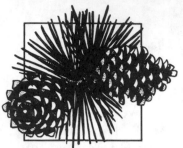

EXPOSURE

Warm-up: John 8:1–11

*Neither do I condemn
you . . . go now and
leave your life of sin
(John 8:10–11).*

Years ago when I was a much younger man, an older friend of mine tried to dissuade me from an activity he considered sinful. "What would Jesus say if He returned and found you there?" he asked.

It's a good question—one worth asking from time to time. What if Jesus caught you smoking pot? What if He returned and found you at an X-rated movie? What if He found you in bed with another's wife? What would He say? Actually, we know what He would say if He caught us in sin. It happened once.

It was one of those days! Jesus was going about His business, trying to teach, when He was interrupted by shouts and sounds of scuffling. A group of clergymen barged in on His class and unceremoniously dumped a woman, disheveled and defiant, at His feet. They said dramatically, "Teacher, this woman was caught in the act of adultery. In the Law Moses commanded us to stone such women. Now what do you say?" (John 8:4–5).

Catapulting the woman into the crowd, the clergy shouted her sin for all to hear. Clearly they had no compassion for her; she was trash. Disdain for her flowed out of them like the tide. And just as certainly no passion for justice existed. Their motive was malice; they wanted to entrap Jesus. The woman was only bait.

They had a closed case. The Law was clear; adultery then was a capital offense (Lev. 20:10; Deut. 22:22). Their innuendo was plain. "*Moses* commanded us to stone such women. Now what do *you* say?" (v. 5, italics mine). If Jesus took issue with Moses' Law, His critics could legitimately assail Him as a lawbreaker and discredit Him as a teacher. On the other hand, if He upheld the Law's judgment, He would no longer be the sinners' friend. They had Him either way! In chess you'd call their move a "fork."

Ignoring them, Jesus stooped over and started to write with His finger in the dirt. He must have been outraged at the way they unhallowed the woman. When they persisted in their questioning, He straightened up and said to them, "If any one of you is without sin, let him be the first to throw a stone at her" (John 8:7). And stooping down again, He began to write on the ground.

Her accusers slowly drifted away. The older ones first—they had the longest track record of sin—the others later, their silence and withdrawal a tacit admission of guilt. And Jesus was left alone with the woman. Looking up He said, "Dear lady, where are they? Has no one condemned you?" She replied calmly, respectfully, "No one, sir." And Jesus said, "Then neither do I condemn you. Go now and leave your life of sin" (vv. 10–11, paraphrase).

Jesus didn't overlook her sin; He called her adultery sin. He knew the harm and heartbreak of it, and He upheld the Law. An adulterous life-style is what Jesus would call a "life of sin," and on another occasion He condemned even lustful thoughts. But God has no heart for throwing stones; judgment is His "alien" work (Isa. 28:21). He longs rather to save, and Jesus is the incarnation of that longing.

The only sinless One, who could throw stones with impunity, did not do so because "God did not send his Son into the world to condemn the world, but to save [it]" (John 3:17). He paid the price for sin so justice could be satisfied and judgment averted; and as Paul later wrote, "There is now no condemnation for those who are in Christ Jesus" (Rom. 8:1).

This woman must have realized from the beginning that Jesus' sympathies were with her and against her accusers. Other men came to use her; this Man had come to save. And save her He did! Not merely from guilt but from sin's power! "Go now," He said, "and leave your life of sin." Her chains fell off; her heart was free.

This story of the fallen woman is what J. R. R. Tolkein would call a "eucatastrophe," where things come right after seeming to go irrevocably wrong. Villains are foiled, people in jeopardy are freed, justice is done, and the ending is happy.

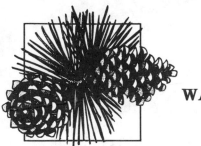

WALKING

Warm-up: Genesis 6

*Noah was a righteous
man, blameless among
the people of his time,
and he walked with God
(Gen. 6:9).*

Noah had a special way of living because he "walked
with God" (Gen. 6:9). To walk with someone signifies
intimacy and companionship; Noah's walk with God
was extraordinary among the men of his time.

Noah had his ordinary days—Monday mornings when
he didn't want to go to work. The ark was a drag, taking
up space in his driveway, trashing up the neighborhood,
amusing and offending his friends. Furthermore, tremendous practical and logistical problems had to be solved.
No one had ever tackled an ark before. But Noah stayed
with the project, building his boat on dry land, far away
from rivers or lakes, while the sun continued to shine,
waiting for one hundred and twenty years for a rainy day.
For this was what God wanted him to do.

Noah not only heard God tell him to build an ark, but
he also "did everything just the way God said" (Gen.
6:22, paraphrase). But I don't think God handed him a list
of things to do each morning. That's just not God's way,
giving us His specs and expectations and demanding that

117

we grind them out. That viewpoint of God badly misses the metaphor of "walking." When in doubt, I think Noah just took a walk with God and talked things over with Him.

Every day Noah took his cares and complaints to God—his big concern over impending catastrophe and his fear for his family and friends. But he also talked with God about the little things—the length of the planks, the height of the partitions, and the pitch with which he made his supership watertight. And later on when he set sail, he and his Friend must have taken a few turns around the deck and talked about the duty roster, the leaks in the hold, and the rations of food and fodder with which he fed his motley boatload of hungry mouths—all the things that might have stressed him out and made him anxious and too intense. No topic was too banal to be brought to God. They walked and talked together about everything and that's what set Noah apart from other men.

St. John of the Cross says that walking with God produces three distinguishing characteristics in men—tranquility, gentleness, and strength. When He's by our side all our actions can be peaceful, gentle, and strong. Which suggests an immense depth of relationship that comes from time spent with our Lord, who "works always in tranquility." Anxiety, intensity, intolerance, instability, pessimism, and every kind of hurry and worry—even on the highest levels, are signs of the man who walks alone, the self-made and self-acting soul. God's men are seldom of that order. They share the quiet and noble qualities of the One with whom they walk.

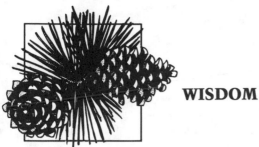

WISDOM

Warm-up: Isaiah 50

Give your servant a discerning heart . . . to distinguish between right and wrong (1 Kings 3:9).

Mule skinners contend that you rarely ever learn anything the *second* time you get kicked by a mule. Having been around both mules and men I have to agree. We don't always get the message from our mistakes. What's needed is wisdom and the gumption to get along without subverting ourselves and others—good sense and sensibility. But where can we go to get that kind of help?

Solomon knew his source. "O LORD my God, you have made your servant king in place of my father David. But I am only a little child and do not know how to carry out my duties. Your servant is here among the people you have chosen, a great people, too numerous to count or number. So give your servant a discerning [Hebrew: "hearing"] heart to distinguish between right and wrong. For who is able to govern this great people of yours?" (1 Kings 3:7–9).

Solomon was a young man, twenty years of age or so, charged with the responsibility of governing one of the most extensive empires in the Ancient Near East. Israel was a dominant power then, her domain extending from the Euphrates to the border of Egypt. Responsible for much, Solomon clearly needed help. And so when God asked the young man what He could do for him (v. 5), Solomon answered well. He asked for wisdom rather than wealth or health.

I always thought God merely increased Solomon's IQ, but now I believe I was wrong. He gave him a "hearing heart" (vv. 9, 11). Wisdom comes from hearing the Word of God. The way to wise up, then, is to listen to God and hear what He has to say.

Wise men go by the Book. They may read many books, but they read all books by the Book. As R. A. Torrey observed: "The truly wise man is he who believes the Bible against the opinions of any man. If the Bible says one thing, and any body of men says another, he will decide, 'This book is the Word of him that cannot lie.'"

Such understanding suggests an apprenticeship of hearing the words of God. The Servant of the Lord, the Messiah, also knew the principle well: "The Sovereign LORD has given me [Christ] an instructed tongue, to know the word that sustains the weary. He wakens me morning by morning, wakens my ear to listen like one being discipled. The Sovereign LORD has opened my ears, and I have not been rebellious; I have not drawn back" (Isa. 50:4–5, paraphrase).

Solomon and the Servant listened reverently and learned their lessons well. It was their wisdom. If they needed to hear God's Word, how much more do we.

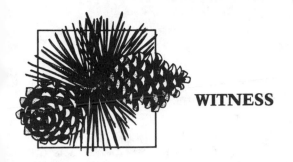

WITNESS

Warm-up: 2 Timothy 2:23–26

*The Lord's servant must
not quarrel (2 Tim. 2:24).*

Christians never seem to fit in. As early as the second century A.D., they had to defend themselves against charges of atheism because they failed to defer to the gods, of incest because they talked about loving their brothers and sisters, of cannibalism because they gathered to "eat" the body of Christ, of being antisocial because they didn't participate in the games, and of being anti-intellectual because in contrast to Plato and his disciples they believed that truth was found in the particulars and not in the universals alone.

Then, as now, Christians found penetrating society difficult. But penetration is the name of the game. Without it, we're good for nothing, like salt that has lost its tang. We've got to mingle more; we've got to gain a greater measure of solidarity with the world and win the right to be heard. Jesus did; He socialized with the irreligious. We tend to cluster too much, to enjoy one another's company at the expense of those outside. Unfortunately, we've not learned from our Lord the principle He taught and exemplified so well. There is no lasting influence without sustained and loving contact.

121

Our standoffish techniques reflect that lack of solid contact. The gospel through bumper stickers, tee shirts, billboards, and lapel buttons may earn us derision but not a hearing. They don't communicate; they alienate. Furthermore, we ought to resist Madison Avenue's invasion of our realm. Witnessing has to do with loving relationships, not sales technique. Thinking in terms of a broad smile and getting one's patter down pat only mechanizes and trivializes the gospel. As John Naisbitt pointed out, the world has gone cold; it needs to be "repersonalized." Most people are looking for someone who cares.

We've got to get natural and down to earth. Tertullian, an early Roman Christian, described witnesses this way: "We [Christians] live among you [non-Christians], eat the same food, wear the same clothes, have the same habits and the same necessities of existence. We are not gymnosophists [a kooky sect encountered in India by Alexander the Great] who dwell in the woods and exile ourselves from ordinary human life. . . . We sojourn with you in the world renouncing neither forum, nor market, nor bath, nor booth, nor workshop, nor inn. . . . We sail with you, we fight with you, we till the ground with you, we join with you in business ventures." Christianity can be lived in the real world of people and things. It has to be lived there to be lived at all. It was meant for the marketplace.

We've also got to find proper ways to talk to our modern friends about God. Traditional words are almost defunct. The problem is familiarity. Most non-Christians have heard the words; they're familiar with the lingo. We need innovative and novel proclamation. Of course, there's nothing novel about the gospel itself. The Good News isn't avante-garde. We don't go on; we go back—

back to Christ and the apostles for our message. But the old message can't be delivered in the same old way.

The language and style of the New Testament in general was not that of classical Greek literature but the language of the common people, the bold, idiomatic street talk of the day. There were no special holy words. Plain speech to common people has always been God's way.

And finally, we must manifest the kindly spirit of the apostle when he wrote: "And the Lord's servant must not quarrel; instead, he must be kind to everyone, able to instruct, not resentful. Those who oppose him he must gently instruct, in the hope that God will grant them repentance leading them to the knowledge of the truth, and that they will come to their senses and escape from the trap of the devil, who has taken them captive to do his will" (2 Tim. 2:24).

There's no need to do fierce battle with non-Christians, no reason to pin them wriggling against the wall. It is, in fact, a sin to be quarrelsome and argumentative. Although we may have to enter into controversy, as our Lord did, woe to the man who enjoys it. Unfortunately, some of us are always spoiling for a fight and are like the man who stopped to watch a street fight and inquired, "Is this a private fight or can anyone join in?"

Sad to say, the fighting is sometimes dirty—name calling and verbal abuse. Discussion and debate on the facts is one thing; personal attack and insult is another. When we resort to innuendo and verbal grenades, we've already lost our moral and rational force. We are like those who rebutted Jesus' well reasoned arguments with the cheap shot: "We [at least] are not born of fornication" (John 8:41, paraphrase).

And so we must avoid what Paul calls "foolish and stupid arguments" (2 Tim. 2:23), and rather be courteous in our demeanor ("kind to everyone"), intelligent and relevant in our declaration of truth ("able to teach"), and non-defensive in our posture ("not resentful"), gently instructing those who oppose "in the hope that God will grant them repentance leading them to a knowledge of the truth, and that they will come to their senses and escape from the trap of the devil, who has taken them captive to do his will" (v. 25).

Those who oppose are not the enemy; they are the victims of the enemy, duped by him to do his will. They have been captivated by Satan, but truth linked with love may deliver them.

Manner and message are inextricably linked; one necessarily goes with the other. Truth alone is not enough. Without grace truth is mere dogma and in the end hardens and brutalizes. And, of course, love can never stand alone. Without truth it becomes mere sentimentalism. Thus there are two liberating elements: truth and love. Only truth delivered with courtesy has power to change an opponent's mind. Apparently, the Good News only sounds good when announced with good manners.

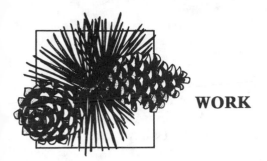

WORK

Warm-up: 2 Thessalonians 3:6–15

*Whatever you do, work
at it with all your heart,
as working for the Lord,
not for men (Col. 3:23).*

If you're like most men, you probably need a good reason
to get up on Monday morning and go to work. Your tasks
may be menial and mindless, offering little challenge or
stimulation. The sameness of it all has taken away any
good reason for doing what you do. What you need is a
philosophy of work that will get you going in the morning.

We labor in a fallen world. The ground works hard
because it's cursed (Gen. 3:17–19). Creation grinds on in
discord, our enemy more often than our ally, and no
amount of work can change that much. Trying to beat
the effects of the Fall simply turns us into workaholics.
We think someday our labor will pay off, but it never
does. Thorns and thistles keep cropping up in our field.

Sin makes everyone and everything more difficult;
other men become our competitors, bent on grabbing our
chips. They want to beat us out of our hard-earned money.

And apart from what sin has done to others, it's done
something to us. We've got a lazy streak. R & R is more
important than work. If we work at all, it's to have more

leisure, more time in our boat or our condo. Work is merely to buy more time away from work.

Because we've mostly left God out of our lives, work has become our substitute for security and significance. Our feelings of self-worth are tied to our work. That's why upward mobility is so important; more pay and greater prestige make us feel better about ourselves. And that's why failure is so devastating to our egos.

But regeneration changes how we perceive ourselves in relation to our work. We begin to learn that security and significance come from God, not what we do. We're special apart from the work we do. He loves us even if we're out of work. And when we begin to see ourselves as He sees us, we don't need work to feel worthy. Then, work becomes valuable, not as a means to an end but as an end in itself.

Work is valuable in itself because God works. He's a hard worker and One who does His work well. He's known for His work. When we too do our work well, when our craftsmanship is sound and our products are well constructed and worthwhile, we're more like God.

Trivial and shoddy work, done solely for profit, diminishes us as men and makes us less manly. Money costs too much when we have to make it that way. We should ask of a job, "Is it any good?" rather than "What does it pay?" And we should ask about a finished product, "Is it worth buying?" rather than "How can I get people to buy it?" As Dorothy Sayers said, "Serve the work! If your heart is not wholly in the work, the work will not be good—and work that is not good serves neither God nor the community; it only serves Mammon."

Work is valuable in itself because work can be service rendered to God. In all our work, we work for Him, and no service rendered to Him is trivial. He sees and it matters to Him. This gives worth to everything we do, even those things no one else notices or appreciates. Michelangelo, painting in some dark corner on the Sistine ceiling, was asked by his helper why he was investing so much time and effort in a part of the painting that no one would ever see. "God will see!" he said.

The job we left last Friday remains the same, but it can have new meaning on Monday morning. Our work is significant no matter what we do. We work because God does; we're more like Him when we do. And we're working for our Lord, an employer who sees and approves. In this frame of mind, we can whistle while we work.

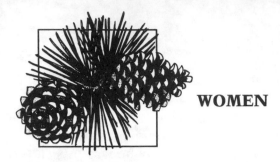

WOMEN

Warm-up: Genesis 1:24–31

*Male and female he
created them (Gen.
1:27).*

There's the bumper sticker that reads: "On the sixth day God created man and rested. Then he created woman and no one has rested ever since." We see the sticker, wince, and then weep for the woman or women in that man's life. You can just hear Archie Bunker saying, "Men are worth more than women! Everybody knows that." But that's not the way a real man ought to think about a woman.

There *are* men who think that way, and even more tragic are the Christian men who've been duped into believing that God puts a premium on being a man, and it turns up in the way they treat their women.

The church may be partly to blame, teaching submission in a form our Lord never intended. The headship of husbands is clearly taught in the Scriptures, but some well-meaning expositors may have turned headship into nothing more than male dominance. A thorough rethinking of the issue is in order.

The Bible teaches that women are as valuable as men. Moses put it this way:

God created man in his own image,
In the image of God he created him;
Male and female he created them. . . .

"Be fruitful and increase in number;
Fill the earth and subdue it.
Rule over [it]" (Gen. 1:27–28).

One aspect of Hebrew poetry is parallelism in which each successive line intensifies the meaning of the preceding line. Thus the poem begins with man's nobility and then leads us to the conclusion that *mankind* is meant—man viewed as male and female. In other words, men and women are both created in God's image and therefore are the most Godlike beings in the universe and in God's eyes have equal worth.

Furthermore, man and woman were both given the mandate to rule: "God blessed *them* and said to *them*. . . . rule over the fish of the sea and the birds of the air and over every living creature that moves on the ground" (Gen. 1:28, italics mine). God's order to subdue the earth was not given to man alone. Women don't go along just for the ride. They too share the mandate to bring the earth under mankind's rule. Another abused text is Genesis 2:18, "It is not good for man to be alone. I will make a helper suitable for him." The Hebrew text actually says that God provided "a helper according to his need." His need was for someone to share the load; his task of subduing the earth was too great to be accomplished alone. And so He gave man a *helper*—a word often used of God Himself, who is our "help." (In Ugaritic, a related Semitic language, the same word means "one who comes to save.") Man's helper is not one who runs and fetches—a gofer—but one who rescues him from working alone. She is his co-laborer, his side-kick.

If men and women then were created equal and share God's mandate to rule, they should be treated with proper respect. Men who treat their women like children by monitoring their activities, curbing their creativity, restricting their freedoms and using them for their own ends are not leading, they're dominating. No wonder women are disaffected; no wonder the feminists rage!

When men in the church or in our culture belittle women or treat them with disdain, or when they think that women, simply because they're women, are troublesome or shallow, weak under pressure, and unreliable with sensitive issues or frivolous with money or time, they've missed what's being said in Scripture and they've mistook the spirit of our Lord.

About forty years ago Dorothy Sayers wrote a remarkable essay entitled "Are Women Human?" She observed: "They [women] had never known a man like this man [Jesus]—there had never been such another. A prophet and teacher who never nagged at them, never flattered or coaxed or patronized [them] . . . who rebuked without querulousness and praised without condescension; who took their questions and arguments seriously; [and] who had no axe to grind and no uneasy male dignity to defend; who took them as he found them and was completely unself-conscious. There is no act, no sermon, no parable in the whole Gospel that borrows its pungency from female perversity; nobody could possibly guess from the words and deeds of Jesus that there was anything 'funny' about woman's nature."

Jesus took women seriously and so should we. They are not subsets of Christian men, nor are they disciplettes of

Christ. They can be grown-up believers, fully man's equal in their capacity to know God, learn from Him, and grow in grace. Paul declares that in terms of Christ's call to discipleship there is "neither male or female" (Gal. 3:28). The differences between the sexes ultimately make no difference at all. And Peter refers to men and women as joint heirs of the grace of life (1 Pet. 3:7, KJV). For a man to think any less of a woman is both unmanly and ungodly.

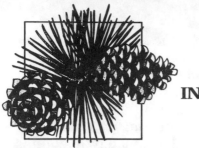

INTENTIONS

Warm-up: Psalm 103

*The LORD is compassion-
ate and gracious, slow to
anger, abounding in love.
He will not always
accuse, nor will he
harbor his anger forever
(Ps. 103:8–9).*

When I gather with my friends and we talk about our
motorcycles, we usually discourse on why we gave them
up. Most of us agree that the best way to get over riding a
bike is to have one; sooner or later you have a good reason to quit.

One of my friends said he gave up biking one day about
thirty feet off the ground. He mistook a gravel pit for the
top of a hill and decided halfway down that he was much
too old for the sport. I gave bikes up for a less dramatic
reason, but my resolve was no less firm.

Carolyn always felt I had the best bike a man could
possibly have. It almost never ran. I was working on it
one evening in the garage and had it partially dismantled
when I realized I needed to buy a part. While I was gone,
my oldest son, who was helping me, decided to crank it
over a couple of times. The gas line was disconnected
(the spark was not), and the bike burst into flames.

Caroyln heard the commotion in the garage and ran to the rescue. She had somewhere read that you shouldn't put water on a gasoline fire, so she grabbed a five-pound bag of flour and dumped it on the bike. She put out the fire and saved the garage; but she magically transformed my dirt bike into a gigantic biscuit. Having heard her mutter a few times about what she would like to do to my bike, I had no doubt that she would have done it if she could; I just didn't know that she could.

I was amazed! The flour wasn't caked on; it was baked on like a concrete shroud. I was so disconcerted that I gave the bike to a friend. For a long time he didn't even know that it was a motorcycle; he thought I had given him the world's largest angel food cake. That was seven years ago; I haven't been on a bike since. I haven't even had the urge.

I still remember our conversation that night after the bike and I cooled down a bit. I asked Carolyn why she put out the fire with flour. "Well," she said a little defensively, "it worked, didn't it?" She was right, of course, but I could only think of Pyrrhus' historic words after the battle of Ausculum in which he decimated his army, "One more such victory and I am lost."

But then, I couldn't stay mad. I know Carolyn too well; she was only trying to help. And I thought of something Paul said: "Judge nothing before the appointed time; wait till the Lord comes. He will bring to light what is hidden in darkness and will expose the motives of men's hearts" (1 Cor. 4:5).

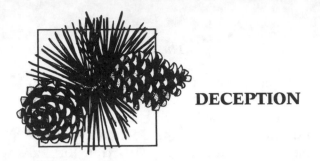

DECEPTION

Warm-up: 2 Chronicles 18:1–34

*Jehoshaphat asked, "Is
there not a prophet of
the LORD here whom we
can inquire of?"
(2 Chron. 18:6).*

Ahab had a knack for being dead wrong about almost
everything. He decided to recapture the city of Ramoth
Gilead, which meant he had to go to war with Aramea,
with whom he had a non-aggression pact. It was a deed
typical of Israel's fiendish and childish king.

Attacking Ramoth Gilead meant he had to enlist the
help of Jehoshaphat, the king of Judah, who was related
to him by marriage. On the occasion of a state visit, he
put the question to his fellow-regent: "Will you go with
me against Ramoth Gilead?" (2 Chron. 18:3). Jehoshaphat was inclined to say yes, but he asked if Ahab had
sought God's will in the matter. Ahab declared that he
had and trotted out his prophets to confirm it: "Go for
it!" they agreed. "God will give it into the king's hand"
(18:5, paraphrase). The encouragement was a lie, but it
was what Ahab loved to hear.

Jehoshaphat was no fool; he knew Ahab's prophets were
stooges. "Is there not a prophet of the LORD here whom we
can inquire of?" Jehoshaphat asked (18:6). "There is still

134

one man," Ahab reluctantly agreed, "but I hate him because he never prophesies anything good about me, but
always bad. He is Micaiah son of Imlah" (18:7).

And so they summoned Micaiah, whom they warned
to conform. But Micaiah, unlike Ahab's prophets, was
God's man and refused to yield: "As surely as the LORD
lives," he announced, "I can tell him only what my God
says" (18:13).

At first Micaiah predicted success, which Ahab immediately dismissed because Micaiah seldom agreed with
his prophets. He called upon Micaiah to tell him "nothing but the truth in the name of the Lord," whereupon
Micaiah laid his life on the line with a poem:

> I saw Israel scattered on the hills
>   like sheep without a shepherd,
> and the LORD said, "These people have no master.
>   Let each one go home in peace."

And then Micaiah drew Ahab a picture: "Hear the
word of the LORD: I saw the LORD sitting on his throne
with all the hosts of heaven standing on his right and on
his left. And the LORD said, 'Who will lure Ahab king of
Israel into attacking Ramoth Gilead and going to his
death there?' One suggested this and another that. Finally, a spirit came forward, stood before the LORD and
said, 'I will lure him.' 'By what means?' the LORD asked.
'I will go and be a lying spirit in the mouths of all his
prophets,' he said. 'You will succeed in luring him,' said
the LORD. 'Go and do it.' So now the LORD has put a lying
spirit in the mouths of these prophets of yours. The LORD
has decreed disaster for you" (2 Chron. 18:18–22).

Ahab should have stopped his plan immediately. He
chose, however, to believe his lying prophets and to have

Micaiah imprisoned until he returned. "If you ever return safely," was Micaiah's laconic reply (18:27).

Ahab went into battle the next morning, disguising himself as a foot soldier to escape detection. But "someone drew his bow at random and hit the king of Israel between the sections of his armor" (18:33). That evening at sunset Ahab, king of Israel, died.

Lucky shot, we say, "that power which erring men call Chance," but which, when closely examined, proves to be the choice of God. Ahab's disaster was decreed. He perished because he was devoted to the lie. He didn't love the truth. So God, consenting to Ahab's deception, permitted a demon to lead him further astray. He was given the lie he loved.

The apostle Paul wrote about other men who "perish because they refused to love the truth and so be saved. For this reason God sends them a powerful delusion so that they will believe the lie and so that all will be condemned who have not believed the truth but have delighted in wickedness" (2 Thess. 2:10–12).

God Himself is not a deceiver. He cannot lie. He will, however, let a man have what he wants if he wants it badly enough. When we take delight in wickedness, God will give us what we want, which is why we get to be such fools. Doing without truth is inevitably our undoing.

The way to avoid deception is to care for truth, for God will give us what we love.

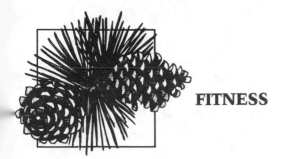

FITNESS

Warm-up: Proverbs 31:10–31

Charm is deceptive, and beauty is fleeting; but a woman [and a man] who fears the LORD is to be praised (Prov. 31:30).

I'm weary of the flap over fitness. First there were the slimming books and then the emphasis shifted to fitness and aerobics. Apparently, thin is now spiritually in, and, Paul not withstanding, exercise profits *much*.

We're told by some Christians that being fit and slender is a matter of self-control, but control may have nothing to do with it. Some of my friends can eat most folks under the table and never gain an ounce. Others are very controlled—eat well and in moderate amounts—but easily gain weight. It's a matter of metabolism and the body God gave us. How can one curse what God has crafted?

Some make weight gains a matter of gluttony, which they may be. Gluttony is one of the seven deadly sins. But it's likewise a form of gluttony to be preoccupied with food, obsessed with one's diet, insisting that food be prepared just so, refusing to eat certain foods even if we cause others embarrassment or undue effort.

For a man to be obsessed with shapeliness and dieting is nothing more than worldliness—conformity to the world. The preferred size and shape of the human body is a matter of convention and conventions are established by our culture or what the Bible would call "the world." The Bible sets no absolutes—says absolutely nothing about the merits of being thin.

There are some serious problems with prizing size over substance. In the first place it's backwards. The body has taken over the spirit. Paul insists that godliness comes before shapeliness because, while "physical training is of some value, . . . godliness has value for all things, holding promise for both the present life and the life to come" (1 Tim. 4:8).

Furthermore, an improper emphasis on the body leads men astray and guides them away from good marriages. Current trends stress a woman's charm and beauty rather than her fear of God (Prov. 31:30). That emphasis can produce a lot of misery later on. Leotards can be a cover-up for foolishness and falseness, laziness and littleness of mind. God's man should rather "acquire a wife in a way that's honorable—not in mere passion like men who don't know God" (1 Thess. 4:5, paraphrase). They should seek those lasting inner qualities that make for truly beautiful women and enduring marriages.

The trend toward thin also leads women astray. Besides contributing to eating disorders it sets them up for a fall. Years ago C. S. Lewis observed that the demons have directed our taste toward an illusion: "We now teach men to like women whose bodies are scarcely distinguishable from those of boys. . . . Since this is a kind of beauty even more transitory than most, we thus aggravate the female's chronic horror of growing old."

Women are being frightened out of contentment with themselves into desiring something that doesn't exist—

being something more (or less) than nature permits a full-grown woman to be. Better that we should encourage a woman to believe that her beauty is the imperishable beauty of the inner self, "the unfading beauty of a gentle and tranquil spirit, which is of great worth in God's sight. For this is the way the holy women of old, who put their trust in God, used to make themselves beautiful" (1 Pet. 3:4, paraphrase).

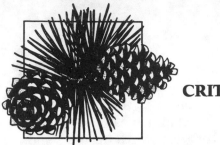

CRITICISM

Warm-up: Galatians 6:1–5

Brothers, if someone is caught in a sin, you who are spiritual should restore him gently. But watch yourself, or you also may be tempted (Gal. 6:1).

A man once unloaded on me that I was a wicked "shepherd who was destroying and scattering the sheep." Those were his exact words. I asked him if he knew that he was quoting Scripture. He said he did. I asked him if he knew by whom it was said and about whom. He didn't. At that point I told him it was the prophet Jeremiah who first said it (23:1) and that it was said about each of Judah's last four kings, Zedekiah, Shallum, Jehoiakim, and Coniah, four of the worst men that ever lived. I thought that would change his mind about me but it didn't.

The best of Christianity is sometimes swallowed up by the worst, and often I think the worst is mean-spirited attacks upon our brothers. It must make outsiders think that becoming a Christian, like meeting Circe, can turn someone into a swine. Something needs to be said to our critics.

Our Lord was very clear about what to do if you have something against another person. He said, "go and show him [your brother] his fault," and settle the matter "just between the two of you" (Matt. 18:15). The best way to handle a complaint against another is frontally. Though it may hurt initially, your loving concern can restore your relationship.

Proverbs says that a faithful friend will wound if he must (Prov. 27:6). A real friend, as Ambrose Bierce observed, "is someone who stabs us in the front." But we should make our thrust "in a spirit of gentleness," aware of our own shortcomings (Gal. 6:1). Correction is much easier to take if offered in humility and love.

Critics need to lighten up, but the criticized need to *toughen up*. We mustn't let our detractors drive us to depression and despair. Every critique provides an opportunity to grow. Forget the critic; it's far more important to consider the criticism, especially if it comes from more than one source. As the old Yiddish proverb concludes, "If one man calls you an ass, pay him no mind; but if two men call you an ass, go get a saddle."

Even if the criticism is unjust, it will still do us some good because living entails learning how to suffer injustice successfully. They nailed Jesus to the cross. You can count on the fact that you'll someday be nailed to the wall!

We should see the ordeal as being crucified with Christ and remember His words: "Not my will but yours be done." As Kierkegaard said, "we must will one will." That's what it means to die. Occasionally it will be His will to bruise us because suffering makes us what He intends us to be. The hurting makes us sweeter, more mellow, and much easier to live and work with because we learn to let go of what we want.

Every humiliation is an opportunity to humble ourselves. God's hands squeeze us to make fine wine. As Peter explained, "Humble yourselves . . . under God's mighty hand, that he may lift you up in due time" (1 Pet. 5:6).

Christ's words from the cross "Father, forgive them, for they do not know what they are doing" remind us that our critics may not know about the hurt they're inflicting on us. Like those who crucified our Lord, they may sincerely believe they're doing the right thing. We ought to forgive them, just as Jesus did, even before they know better.

Our response should go beyond mere forgiveness to blessing and reconciliation. As Paul said, "when we are cursed, we bless; . . . when we are slandered, we try to conciliate" (1 Cor. 4:12–13, paraphrase). Jesus declared we ought to love our enemies and pray for those who persecute us (Matt. 5:44). Anyway, bitterness only afflicts us, not those who afflict us.

When Jesus was at the end of His tether, He cried out, "Father, into your hands I commit my spirit" (Luke 23:46). When we reach the end of our resources, we, like our Lord, must put ourselves in God's hands. We can explain ourselves, though ultimately we can't defend or justify ourselves nor should we try. We don't have to answer every charge. We're guarded by God. As the proverb puts it, "Do not say, 'I'll pay you back for this wrong!' Wait for the Lord, and he will deliver you" (Prov. 20:22).

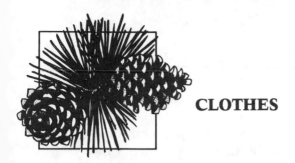

CLOTHES

Warm-up: James 2:1–13

*Clothe yourselves with
the Lord Jesus Christ
(Rom. 13:14).*

Christian thought sometimes runs amok, ignoring mountains and making too much of molehills, so it may seem trivial to theologize on bibs and tuckers. Yet if we think about our faith at all, we have to think about clothes, since in our culture all men wear them.

In this fad-mad world, ad men get to us, creating artificial needs to sell us more of their goods. Madison Avenue trades on our male egos by appeals to manliness, snobbery, and forced obsolescence. They entice our sense of pride, and we fall in line. Like Piglet and Pooh, we follow one another's footprints around the tree. We shouldn't be fooled by that ruse.

Pride plays a role in the way we dress, but so does sexuality. Clothing does and should accentuate sexuality, but dressing to emphasize sexuality differs from dressing to stimulate another sexually. As Kris Rudell, a colleague of mine pointed out, "Dressing to accent sexuality lies about one's availability and reinforces the confusion in our culture concerning the role of and context for sexual intimacy." It's unloving to intentionally dress in a way that causes others to stumble into sin.

What is proper clothing for a man? There are no easy answers, but I think in most cases it's good to dress *down* rather than up. Advertisements entice us to be noticed, but God's man has a fundamentally different motivation: He wants to be clothed with humility. This means we should normally dress to blend in and not attract attention to ourselves, which generally means that we dress conventionally, the way most people would dress on a given occasion. Being daring, weird, and way out, draws attention to us. On the other hand, being deliberately frumpy or way out of fashion can also put all eyes on us, although I agree with John White that dowdiness is not the great spiritual tragedy some people think it is.

When others think of us, we hope they remember us by the character of Christ seen in us and not by the cut of our clothes. Being a clothes-horse misses the point. As Augustine taught his students, "Do not attract attention by the way you dress. Endeavor to impress by your manner of life, not by the clothes you wear." Better that we adorn ourselves with humility; better that we decrease and our Lord increase.

On the other hand, though we may not want to be seen, we do want to be heard. The two are actually related. Life is governed by stock reactions and first impressions are often formed by dress. If we're unkempt and untidy or too casually dressed for an occasion, it may prevent others from taking us seriously. Too innovative or avant-garde garb can produce the same result.

Clothes shouldn't matter; we shouldn't size up others by their "flesh," but some do (2 Cor. 5:16). Therefore, rather than hinder another, we should dress in a manner that will not offend. As Paul said in several texts, the Kingdom of God is not eating or drinking or exercising our freedom to dress as we please but seeking righteousness and peace. Why would we let a trivial thing like clothes prevent another from hearing the Good News? Love will never let clothes stand in the way.

The bottom line is love. Love dictates dress. It's unloving to dress to intentionally stimulate another. It's unloving to dress in a manner that attracts attention to us and away from others. It's unloving to dress in a way that hinders others from seeing our Lord and hearing about Him. In the end, it's the love of Christ that teaches us how to dress.

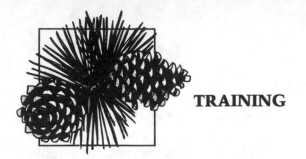

TRAINING

Warm-up: Philippians 3:7–21

*Train yourself to be
godly (1 Tim. 4:7).*

Paul must have been an athlete, at least a would-be athlete. He certainly kept in shape. Trekking back and forth across the Roman Empire, he walked more miles in a few years than most of us walk in a lifetime. I calculated once that he logged over fifty thousand miles, which is more than the average postman does in a lifetime. He must have had legs like a Sherpa.

He also frequently used athletic metaphors in his letters. Most of us illustrate from our personal disciplines, and I assume Paul did the same.

In one place he reminded a young friend that an athlete wins no prize "unless he competes according to the rules" (2 Tim. 2:5). Paul, no doubt, was referring to the training rules of his day that required strenuous conditioning and physical fine-tuning before a contest. No random exercise regimens were allowed. The "Rules of the Games" mandated that only the fittest could compete, a practice that led to excellence. It still rings true today. You can't be unregulated and hope to excel; discipline is the name of the game.

In another letter Paul explained how to pursue excellence with track and boxing examples. "Do you not know that in a race all the runners run, but only one gets the prize? Run in such a way as to get the prize. Everyone who competes in the games goes into strict training. They do it to get a crown [a fading leaf] that will not last; but we do it to get a crown that will last forever. Therefore I do not run like a man running aimlessly; I do not fight like a man beating the air. No, I beat my body and make it my slave so that after I have preached to others, I myself will not be disqualified for the prize" (1 Cor. 9:24–27).

Boxing in those days was a brutal sport, mostly bare-fisted or worse (they sometimes wrapped their fists with rawhide strips). Matches lasted until one of the fighters was down and definitely out! There were no draws; someone always left the ring feet first.

The word *beat* is a technical term for a particular kind of punch—a shot under the eye that usually put one's opponent on the canvas for keeps. Apparently, Paul alluded here to the accepted training practice of toughening one's face by a series of self-inflicted blows. His point is graphically clear. If you want to win, you have to suffer; pain is a corollary of progress.

Paul knew and apparently approved of the training routines of his day. He understood their value. Perhaps he practiced them. But he put all things physical in perspective when he wrote to Timothy: "Physical training is of some value, but godliness has value for all things" (1 Tim. 4:8).

Timothy may have pumped iron like many young men did in the Greco-Roman world. Paul agreed that these workouts had "some value." The pursuit of fitness is good but the pursuit of God is the greater good because it makes us fit for this life and for the life to come. Muscles come and go, but godliness goes on forever.

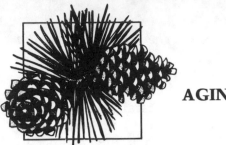

AGING

Warm-up: Psalm 71

You, however, will go to your fathers in peace and be buried at a good old age (Gen. 15:15).

Some men grow old gracefully. Age softens their faces; they get sweeter as the days go by, while others get sour and unsociable. It's important to know why we get one way or the other because all of us are getting older every day.

Old age can be "good old age" as the Old Testament says, or it can be very bad; it depends on the route we take. As Thomas à Kempis said, "Of what use is a long life if we amend it so little? Alas, a long life often adds to our sins rather than to our virtue."

That's why old folks seem to us to be either more irascible and impossible as they age or they get sweeter and easier to live with than ever before. Certain traits don't develop simply because men get old. There are conditions that cause confusion and anxiety as we age, but nothing inherent in aging shapes or changes our character, impairs us morally, and makes us mean. As we grow old we become what we've been becoming all along.

Paul was right again: "A man reaps what he sows" (Gal. 6:7). No one has beat the law of inevitable consequence. In the end we get what we've been growing all along. Every time we sow to the sinful nature we begin to decay. Every time we pander to the flesh we sow the seeds of our own destruction. On the other hand, every time we till the soil of the Spirit we grow more like God. Every decision based on truth makes us more alive than ever before.

C. S. Lewis concluded: "Every time you make a choice, you are turning the central part of you, the part that chooses, into something a little different than it was before. And taking your life as a whole with all your innumerable choices, all your life long you are slowly turning this central thing either into a heavenly creature or into a hellish creature; either a creature that is in harmony with God and with other creatures and with itself or else into one that is in a state of war and hatred with God and with its fellow creatures and with itself. To be the one kind of creature is heavenly . . . it is joy and peace and knowledge and power; to be the other means madness, horror, idiocy, rage, impotence and loneliness. Each of us, at each moment, is progressing to the one state or the other."

We need not wither and decay. Aging doesn't necessarily mean deterioration. We can get it back! We can start afresh; old dogs *can* learn new tricks. Even if early on we emptied our life of God, we can ask Him to fill us again. No one is too far gone.

O Savior! Has thy grace declined?
Can years affect the Eternal Mind?
Or time its love destroy?

Every day can be a new beginning toward "good old age." It can mean maturing, growing in grace and becoming more like Jesus, getting "sweeter as the days go by." There's something exquisitely manly about an older man who is "stayed upon Jehovah," filled with His presence, and redolent with His fragrance.

The righteous will flourish like a palm tree,
they will grow like a cedar of Lebanon;
Planted in the house of the Lord,
they will flourish in the courts of our God.
They will still bear fruit in old age,
They will stay fresh and green,
proclaiming, "the LORD is upright;
he is my Rock, and there is no wickedness in
     him" (Ps. 92:12–15).

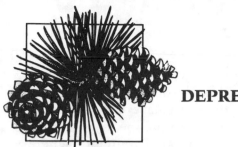

DEPRESSION

Warm-up: 1 Kings 19:1–21

I have been very zealous for the LORD God Almighty. The Israelites have rejected your covenant, broken down your altars, and put your prophets to death with the sword. I am the only one left, and now they are trying to kill me too (1 Kings 19:10).

Elijah came out of the backwoods of Israel, garbed in a turned-out sheepskin coat, living off the land, playing havoc with the religious and political establishment in Israel. He was King Ahab's nemesis.

Ahab, the monarch of Elijah's era, was the worst of Israel's kings. He joined Israel to idols through a political alliance, made by a royal marriage, with neighboring Phoenicia. Ahab and Israel got the murderous Jezebel.

When Jezebel moved to Jezreel, Israel's capital city, she brought along her Phoenician gods and goddesses—the Baalim and the Ashteroth—the most corrupt pantheon ever devised. Sex orgies and child sacrifice were the name of the game. Baalism was deemed evil even by the Romans, who encountered the same god at Carthage and

151

who, though hardly paragons of virtue themselves, were utterly grossed out by it. This was Jezebel's faith.

When Jezebel moved into the palace she moved in! There was no question about who wore the royal pants in the family. Baalism became the state religion, whereupon Elijah began his flaming duel with Ahab and Jezebel and their debased, debasing religion.

Mount Carmel was the climax (1 Kings 18), a classic shoot-out with Elijah taking on Jezebel's clergy at outrageous odds and soundly thrashing them. Ah, the thrill of victory! Exhilarated by his triumph, Elijah ran ahead of Ahab's chariot all the way to Jezreel, a distance of about twenty-five miles. Delusions of grandeur danced in his head—perhaps a court chaplaincy. Who could know what good things lay ahead!

When Ahab reported the debacle to Jezebel she sent a messenger to Elijah with this terse verse: May the gods get me, If I don't get you!

Elijah ran for his life to Beersheba, about seventy miles from Jezebel, where he dropped from exhaustion under a broom tree and prayed that he might die. "Enough is enough," he said (19:3–5). Elijah was bummed out.

I understand. Most of us get discouraged at times. We have off-days, blue Mondays, and bouts with the blahs. Depression is more chronic for others, and the mood shifts are more acute and troublesome. Depression, mild or severe, is a pervasive malady. We can understand Elijah, his apathy and self-pity, his loss of self-worth, and even his self-destructive bent. More important, we can learn from his recovery.

God doesn't say much at first. He fed his man and gave him a chance to sleep. Then the Lord "came back a second time and touched him and said, 'Get up and eat for the journey is too much for you.' So he got up and ate and drank. Strengthened by that food, he traveled forty days and forty nights until he reached Horeb, the mountain of God" (19:7–8).

Fatigue was a factor in Elijah's gloom. Over-wrought and underfed, he had abused his body. So God, who made man and knows him best of all, arranged for some R&R. In the strength of that rest, Elijah journeyed to Horeb, where God spoke to the deeper elements of his misery.

At Horeb, the place of revelation, Elijah "went into a cave and spent the night. And the word of the LORD came to him: 'What are you doing here, Elijah?'" (Why aren't you still in the thick of things?) Elijah replied, "'I have been very zealous for the LORD God Almighty. The Israelites have broken down your altars, and put your prophets to death with the sword. I am the only one left, and now they are trying to kill me too'" (19:9–10).

Disillusionment is the child of illusion. Elijah expected God to make short work of Jezebel. He figured the Almighty might waste her with a bolt from the blue. Elijah's unrealistic expectations led to disappointment. Disappointment, brooded over, bred self-pity, which, indulged in, made him blue.

It's easy to get down. The hard part is to get up, an effort even Elijah seemed unwilling to attempt. But God would not let Elijah languish. He said, "Go out and stand on the mountain . . . for the LORD is about to pass by" (19:11). There the Lord gave Elijah a lesson in His ways.

God's revelation began with brute force—winds of hurricane velocity, a titanic earthquake, a terrifying electrical storm. In each circumstance God was conspicu-

153

ously absent. But then came a gentle breeze, the sign of God's subtle presence.

We can never know about God. We can't predict His way of working and we can't dictate to Him the time or the terms of deliverance. He does things His way. "Anyone who thinks he has the ways of God conveniently tabulated, analyzed and correlated with convenient glib answers . . . [for] aching hearts has not gone far in this maze of mystery we call life and death. . . . He has no stereotyped way of doing what he does. I accept what he does, how he does it" (Vance Havner).

God quashed the Baalites on Carmel with a thunderbolt, but he disposed of Jezebel another way. He delivered Peter from prison by an earthquake, but He left His own Son on the cross to die quietly and deliver us all. The bottom line is that God doesn't always tip His hand; we can't always know what He's doing. If we think we can or must, we're destined for disappointment, depression, and despair.

There are no guarantees that we will see God's deliverance and that life will run smoothly, without trauma or trial. Sometimes we'll look foolish and weak. We'll be opposed, evil will hurt us, we'll be misunderstood and maligned. The wheels will drop off our programs and our best-laid plans will "gang aft-agley." But there's something in the wind. Whether we perceive it or not, God is moving quietly, inexorably, to bring about salvation His way, and in His time He will deliver.

Elijah missed the message. When God asked him again, "What are you doing here?" Elijah replied as before. But God's final word was stern and firm, a kindly kick in the rear: "Go back the way you came. . . . Anoint Haziel king over Aram. Also, anoint Jehu . . . king over

Israel, and anoint Elisha . . . to succeed you as a prophet"
(19:13, 15–16). These actions brought a final end to Ahab
and Jezebel and their unholy alliance.

Elijah couldn't snap out of his depression, but he could
choose to act. His emotions may have been immobilized,
but his will was free. He could do what God asked him to
do. His obedience was the beginning of his healing.
"Elijah went from there. . . . " (19:19). He got back in the
thick of things.

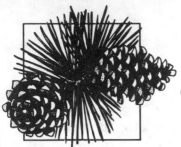

CONCEALMENT

Warm-up: Joshua 7:1–26

*My son, give glory to the
LORD, the God of Israel,
and give him the praise.
Tell me what you have
done; do not hide it from
me (Josh. 7:19).*

Ai was a small stronghold a few miles up the ravine from
the fallen fortress of Jericho. Defended by a small cadre of
Canaanites, it was no big deal.

After the conquest of Jericho, Joshua was advised to
send only a few to assault this insignificant enclave. "'Do
not weary all the people, for only a few men are there.' So
about three thousand men went up; but they were routed
by the men of Ai, who killed about thirty-six of them.
They chased the Israelites from the city gate as far as the
stone quarries and struck them down on the slopes. At
this the heart of the people melted and became like water" (Josh. 7:3–5).

The fight for Ai was a fiasco. Thrown into panic and
hotly pursued, Israel's army retreated down the steep
slopes of the canyon to the quarries near the Jordan
where they found cover in the rocks. Israel lost the
ground they gained at Jericho, and worse yet, lost the
lives of some of their fine young men. It was a debacle
that God's people would never forget.

Joshua, confused and critical of God's performance, fell on his face before the ark: "Why did you ever bring this people across the Jordan to deliver us into the hands of the Amorites to destroy us? If only we had been content to stay on the other side of the Jordan! O Lord what can I say, now that Israel has been routed by its enemies?" (7:7–9).

The Lord's response was curt: "Stand up! What are you doing down on your face? [This is no time to pray!] Israel has sinned; they have violated my covenant, which I commanded them to keep. They have taken some of the devoted things; they have stolen, they have lied, they have put them with their own possessions. That is why the Israelites cannot stand against their enemies; they turn their backs and run because they have been made liable to destruction. I will not be with you anymore unless you destroy whatever among you is devoted to destruction" (7:10–12).

The Lord had directed Israel to take no plunder from that wicked place, but someone got greedy. Forbidden fruit was taken. The offender must be discovered and punished if Israel was to stand against her enemies.

Good notions must take advantage of their first ripeness. We mustn't try the Spirit with delays. "Early the next morning Joshua had Israel come forward by tribes, and Judah was taken. The clans of Judah came forward, and he took the Zerahites. He had the clan of the Zerahites come forward by families, and Zimri was taken. Joshua had his family come forward man by man, and Achan, son of Carmi . . . was taken" (7:16–18). Achan's sin had found him out.

Then Joshua said to Achan, pleading as a father would with a wayward child, "'My son, give glory to the LORD, the God of Israel [a solemn vow to tell the truth], and give him the praise [confess your sin]. Tell me what you have done; do not hide it from me.' Achan replied, 'It is true! I have sinned against the LORD, the God of Israel. . . . When I saw in the plunder a beautiful robe from Babylonia, two hundred shekels of silver and a wedge of gold weighing fifty shekels, I coveted them and took them. [If only Achan had waited! God would have given.] They are hidden in the ground inside my tent, with the silver underneath.' So Joshua sent messengers, and they ran to the tent and there it was, hidden in his tent with the silver underneath. They took the things from the tent and brought them to Joshua and all the Israelites and spread them out before the LORD" (7:19–21).

Joshua, together with all Israel, and with heavy heart, took Achan and his treasure to the desert: "Why have you brought this disaster on us? . . ." And they stoned him there, and piled a great heap of stones over his remains. Achan was buried in the rubble of his sin. "Then the LORD turned from his fierce anger. Therefore that place has been called the Valley of Achor [Disaster] ever since" (7:26).

And so it must be: "All that is not beautiful in the beloved, all that comes between and is not of love's kind must be destroyed. For our God is a consuming fire" (George MacDonald).

Sin attracts us like gold and a Babylonian garment attracted Achan. We see, we covet, and we take. We think we'll not go too far. We can sin when it pleases us and pass on. We've bought the lie, the Great Denial: "You will not die!" (Gen. 3:3). And in the end, it is we who are "taken."

Sin can never be hidden, kept in control or in place. "He who commits sin is the slave of sin" (John 8:34). We soon find ourselves controlled by our transgressions, humiliated and mastered by them, dominated by pleasure, commanded by every vice. Augustine said, "The penalty for sin is sin." In time, our sin is known. What we have hidden is shouted aloud from the house-top. Our humiliation has gone public.

God permits our decline. Our downturns are His redemptive wrath, His saving torment to bring us home. He is with us as we flee and fall. He closes in on us, nudging us, warning us, and then, at last, giving us our way until we self-destruct. God is relentless in His judgment: He'll not give up until we're "taken." "It is a matter of indifference to God's grace how abominable you are if you will come to the light. But woe be to you if you will not come to the light" (C. S. Lewis).

We must come to the light. We must not conceal sin or safeguard it. We must take it to the valley and put it to death. We must judge ourselves if we would not be judged by God (1 Cor. 11:31). And when a man repents and turns with disgust from his sin, God is there to lift him up, higher than he ever stood before. The place of judgment becomes a place of new beginnings; the Valley of Achor becomes "a door of hope" (Hos. 2:15).

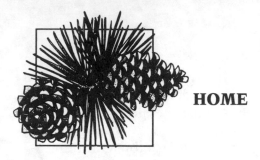

HOME

Warm-up: John 14:1–6

Do not let your hearts be troubled. Trust in God, trust also in me (John 14:1).

Most of my boyhood in Texas was spent in the cedar breaks south of Dallas. The countryside is built up now, but back then it was mostly ranchland, rolling chalk hills, redolent with cedar trees and junipers. The woods were a boy's paradise with wonderful places to explore and pretend. At night, when I was home in bed on our screened-in porch, I'd listen to the coyotes and bobcats and other noises in the woods and exult in the fact that I was home rather than out in the dark where the wild things were.

One of my favorite daytime pastimes was walking the creek. It was a special stream, a kind of oasis in a very dry land. The brook ran clear most of the year and supported lush stands of cottonwoods and willows. When I think about that creek today, I think of deep shade, long walks, solitude and friendly dogs, memories of leaving home early in the morning with my old yellow hound, my single shot .410, a bag lunch that my mother made, walking to the springhead or downstream to where the creek emptied into the lake.

Those hikes were high adventure for me, at least I made it adventure. There were rocks to skip, birds to watch, dams to build, tracks to follow, squirrels to flush along the way. And then if I made it to the mouth of the creek, my dog and I would sit and share our lunch while we watched the biplanes land across the lake.

We'd linger as long as we could, but only so long, for my father wanted me home before the sun went down. The shadows grew long and the hollows got dark fast in the cedar breaks. I'd be wishing along the way that I was already home. Though weary, I'd hurry on. It was the hope of going home that kept me going.

Our house sat on a hill behind some trees, but I could always see the light on the porch as I made my way through the woods in the gathering dusk. The light was always on until all the family was in. Often my father would be sitting on the back porch, reading the newspaper, waiting for me. "How did it go?" he'd ask. "Pretty good," I'd say. "It was a good trip, but it's good now to be home."

It's been a long time since I walked that creek, but the memories live on and they fill me with what Mole in *The Wind and the Willows* called "divine discontent and longing." They make me think of another long and sometimes hard journey, the one I'm making now. But I know that at the end of it there's a caring Father and my eternal home. It's the thought of going home that keeps me going. It sure will be good to get there.

As I look back on my life I must say that it has been good, though it has had its ups and downs. Like John Bunyan's Pilgrim I've gone on "sometimes comfortably, sometimes sighingly," but taken as a whole my journey has been a pretty good trip. One of these days, though, it'll start to get dark and then I'll head for home. I'm expected there. The light is on and the Father is waiting for me. I suppose he'll ask, just like my father used to ask, "How did it go?" "Pretty good," I'll say. "It was a good trip, but it's good to be home—home before dark."

NOTE TO THE READER

The publisher invites you to share your response to the message of this book by writing Discovery House Publishers, Box 3566, Grand Rapids, MI 49501, USA. For information about other Discovery House books, music, or videos, contact us at the same address or call 1-800-653-8333. Find us on the Internet at http://www.dhp.org/ or send e-mail to books@dhp.org.